W9-ATO-724

IMPROVE YOUR

MARKETING

TO GROW YOUR

BUSINESS

Ideas. Action. Impact.
Wharton School Publishing

In the face of accelerating turbulence and change, business leaders and policy makers need new ways of thinking to sustain performance and growth.

Wharton School Publishing offers a trusted source for stimulating ideas from thought leaders who provide new mental models to address changes in strategy, management and finance. We seek out authors from diverse disciplines with a profound understanding of change and its implications. We offer books and tools that help executives respond to the challenge of change.

Every book and management tool we publish meets quality standards set by The Wharton School of the University of Pennsylvania. Each title is reviewed by the Wharton School Publishing Editorial Board before being given Wharton's seal of approval. This ensures that Wharton publications are timely, relevant, important, conceptually sound or empirically based, and implementable.

To fit our readers' learning preferences, Wharton publications are available in multiple formats, including books, audio, and electronic.

To find out more about our books and management tools, visit us at whartonsp.com and Wharton's executive education site, exceed.wharton.upenn.edu.

IMPROVE YOUR MARKETING TO GROW YOUR BUSINESS

INSIGHTS AND INNOVATION THAT DRIVE BUSINESS AND BRAND GROWTH

Hunter Hastings
with Jeff Saperstein

Vice President, Publisher: Tim Moore
Associate Editor-in-Chief and Director of Marketing: Amy Neidlinger
Wharton Editor: Yoram (Jerry) Wind
Acquisitions Editor: Martha Cooley
Editorial Assistant: Pamela Boland
Development Editor: Russ Hall
Digital Marketing Manager: Julie Phifer
Publicist: Amy Fandrei
Marketing Coordinator: Megan Colvin
Cover Designer: Alan Clements
Managing Editor: Gina Kanouse
Project Editor: Anne Goebel
Copy Editor: Gayle Johnson
Proofreader: Megan Wade
Indexer: WordWise Publishing
Compositor: TnT Design, Inc.
Manufacturing Buyer: Dan Uhrig

❚❚❚ Wharton School Publishing

© 2008 by Pearson Education, Inc.
Publishing as Wharton School Publishing
Upper Saddle River, New Jersey 07458
www.whartonsp.com/title/9780132331593

Wharton School Publishing offers excellent discounts on this book when ordered in quantity for bulk purchases or special sales. For more information, please contact U.S. Corporate and Government Sales, 1-800-382-3419, corpsales@pearsontechgroup.com. For sales outside the U.S., please contact International Sales at international@pearsoned.com.

First Printing October 2007

ISBN-13: 978-0-132-33159-3
ISBN-10: 0-13-233159-4

Pearson Education Ltd.
Pearson Education Australia PTY, Limited.
Pearson Education Singapore, Pte. Ltd.
Pearson Education North Asia, Ltd.
Pearson Education Canada, Ltd.
Pearson Educación de Mexico, S.A. de C.V.
Pearson Education—Japan
Pearson Education Malaysia, Pte. Ltd.

Library of Congress Cataloging-in-Publication Data

Hastings, Hunter.
 Improve your marketing to grow your business : insights and innovation
that drive business and brand growth / Hunter Hastings.
    p. cm.
 ISBN 978-0-13-233159-3 (hardback : alk. paper)
 1. Marketing--Management. 2. Information technology. 3. Brand name
products--Marketing. 4. Internet marketing. I. Title.
 HF5415.13.H3654 2008
 658.8--dc22
                                          2007018533

For Julie

Contents

Acknowledgments

I would like to thank Jeff Saperstein, who organized, collaborated, and enhanced the material in its many stages of development.

Thanks to Tam Nguyen and Julie Moy for their assistance in transcribing the interviews.

Many people contributed their time, talents, perspectives, and energy to this project. Special thanks to Larry Huston, Tom O'Toole, Mark McCallum, Mike Keyes, Marci Sapers, Jeff Wysocki, Jim Garrity, Bob DeAngelis, Cheryl Perkins, Oscar Jamhouri, Peter Boland, and Bill Veltrop for their interviews.

We are especially grateful to Tom Falk, CEO of Kimberly-Clark, for his encouragement and his pioneering role in the real business of enterprise marketing management.

A special thanks to my partner, Gordon Wade, whose wit, wisdom, and insight greatly enhanced this book. I wish to acknowledge the help of my colleagues, Sat Duggal and Trini Amador, and also Betsy Farner, the CFO of EMM Group, for her patience and diligence.

Hunter Hastings

About the Author

Hunter Hastings is a marketing veteran with more than thirty years' experience. He is the co-founder and CEO of EMM Group (www.emmgroup.net). He consults with Global 2000 companies on marketing capability development across a wide range of industries, including consumer packaged goods, consumer and business financial services, pharmaceuticals, and consumer and business technology.

Jeff Saperstein is the author of *Creating Regional Wealth in the Innovation Economy*. He is an instructor at San Francisco State University College of Business and a consultant on innovation in marketing and technology. His Web site is www.creatingregionalwealth.com.

Foreword

Organic growth is management's most critical job. For those running well-established businesses and brands, you should look first and foremost to the businesses that you are already in and the brands you already own to get as much growth from those as you can. This organic growth is the highest return on investment available to any company.

Most of us have already cost-cut to maximize the bottom line. There is no way to achieve growth breakthroughs by squeezing out more efficiency. The effort to grow through acquisition has proven to be too difficult, expensive, and risky for most people. Acquisitions require you to manage the unfamiliar, whether it's the change management involved with integration or mastering new categories and businesses. Bigger is not better; better is better!

So the prudent alternative is to do more to mine the growth of the businesses you currently manage. It is possible to defy the perceived boundaries and limitations of your current businesses and break through to new levels of growth.

The way ahead is through new insights into the needs of consumers and channel customers, which in turn lead to innovations. If you enhance benefits rather than merely improving products, your brands and solutions become more significant in the lives of consumers and in the business plans of your customers and partners. Achieving these breakthroughs requires new ways of working and leveraging your knowledge, relationships, and people assets. Today, the successful business leader must make these breakthroughs possible through purposeful changes in the organizational culture.

This level of change includes a radical transformation of what is known as "marketing." Marketing must move to a holistic, system-wide approach that begins with insights and that drives rapidly and relentlessly to the delivery of a better experience to consumers and channel customers in the marketplace. This is a marketing discipline built on process, creativity, measurement, and collaboration.

The principles and practices espoused in this book will help you create the right mind-set for change. All of us need to rethink how we deliver value to our shareholders, customer channels, and consumers while transforming our organizations to be attractive to the best talent, both within and with outside partners. This book will help you steer your organization through an ever more challenging business environment— to thrive, not just survive.

Tom Falk
CEO, Kimberly-Clark Corporation

Preface

Most business executives work for enterprises that are characterized by continuous rather than disruptive business models and practices. Their challenge is not to invent the next Google or eBay, but to meet Wall Street expectations for sustained high levels of top-line revenue growth that generate consistent increases in profitability. Their businesses may have been around for more than 100 years, like Procter & Gamble (P&G), and they seek to emulate that company's performance in coaxing new growth out of old brands. Or it may be a newer business that has started to hit a flatter part of the growth curve, like Microsoft, and is looking to find the next accelerator.

Marketing is the capability that can provide these executives with the engine for growth. We use the word "capability" deliberately to represent a new way of thinking about marketing, much different from how conventional marketing is conceived and practiced. To succeed, management (not just marketing professionals) must adopt a new mind-set for change. This new way of thinking includes the following:

- Reengineering marketing via process, technology, metrics, and new organization forms
- Embedding marketing processes to ensure that business plans reflect vital consumer and customer insights
- Employing marketing technology to unleash creativity, innovation, and growth
- Applying iron discipline to the metrics of the marketing demand creation process

Marketing is no longer a function, but a core competence in growing and sustaining businesses. Major global corporations such as P&G, Wachovia Bank, Hyatt Corporation, Brown-Forman, and Kimberly-Clark have begun to reengineer their concept and practice of marketing to get more growth from every dollar of marketing investment.

EMM Group is prominent among the practitioners who work with these leading companies to successfully implement these new marketing concepts and practices. We provide the case histories of companies in major industries and views of some of the most successful business professionals as they testify to the transformation of their business through the application of marketing processes and the use of the new marketing technology.

This book is about how to engineer marketing—from concept to practical application—to profitably increase growth for existing businesses that need to be ignited for sustained return on investment. We show you what you need to know and how to get it done.

Hunter Hastings

Introduction

A supply-side productivity revolution has transformed business over the past thirty years. Global companies have integrated manufacturing, logistics, finance, and other components into unified global supply chains. By applying process engineering and quantitative process improvement techniques such as lean manufacturing and Six Sigma, companies such as Wal-Mart, Dell, and Toyota have achieved continuous improvement in the operating efficiency of the supply chain. By codifying the processes in software, they have made them available to operators across the globe, who can collaborate via the desktop/laptop/handheld device and the Internet to further reduce cycle times, cut costs, and increase accuracy.

The next revolution in company productivity is coming on the demand side. Demand generation processes can and must be engineered into systems that can be utilized by every company employee. Activities that, in the past, might have been deemed to be beyond such systematic approaches can be the areas of corporate spending that benefit most—including innovation, communications, and demand planning. Supply-side disciplines such as Six Sigma, designed to increase the efficiency of processes after they have been engineered, can be applied on the demand side to seemingly unlikely activities such as generating insights and creating advertising. Every step in every process must be scrutinized by metrics, with the ultimate focus resting on the creation of outputs. In the case of the demand side of the corporation, the outputs are revenue growth, the development of intangible assets, and shareholder value. With the right metrics in place, software and networked technologies drive the productivity of the demand side of the corporation as they have on the supply side, and provide monitoring and measurement to eliminate unpredictable outcomes.

Table I.1 compares the supply-side and demand-side dynamics.

Table I.1   Supply-Side and Demand-Side Dynamics

Supply Side	Demand Side	Comments
Objective: efficiency	Objective: growth	The focus on the demand side is exclusively on driving revenue and profit growth.
Integrated operations management	Knowledge management	Operations management is transactional, aimed at driving speed and efficiency. Knowledge management is collaborative sharing, aimed at leveraging enterprise knowledge to create new value.
Customer-centric operations	Customer insights	A customer orientation is important on the supply side, but customer insights are the critical new ingredient in the process of driving growth.
Multisourcing	Open innovation	Supply chains run most efficiently when the value chain is balanced between what the company does well and what outsourcers do well. Innovation produces more value at a fast speed when it's open, and new ideas and capabilities can come from both inside and outside the company.
Global operations management	Global brand management	Global supply chains have been optimized for global sourcing and logistics. Global brand management must be optimized for the global application of insights.
Technical expertise to manage process	Organization and culture change to manage process	Supply-chain operations solved the organizational barriers to integrated process years ago. Marketing organizations still operate in silos and demonstrate a process that's resistant to culture, and they must overcome this barrier.
Enterprise Resource Planning (ERP) software	Enterprise marketing management software	Software is the answer to pulling together all the integration of operations. On the demand side, enterprise marketing management software links knowledge to insight creation to innovation to marketing and sales programs.

We believe the key to creating growth is to focus the organization on insights into the customer and then guide people and systems in both generating these insights and capitalizing on the best of them. This is done through fast-to-market innovations in products, services, and delivery. At the core, the job of marketing is to build brand equity through these insight-driven innovations. Inherent in this transformation is the new understanding of knowledge management. The marketing function as well as the whole organization must change to harness the power of knowledge to drive growth.

Information Technology Will Reinvent the Marketing Function

Marketing is on the cusp of a radical transformation as information technology (IT) changes the industry. This requires a co-evolution between the new capabilities that technology provides and the mind-set and processes required by the marketing function. Achieving top-line revenue growth and sustaining profitable businesses will depend on the corporate embrace of the reengineering of marketing through new processes to unleash the power that technology affords.

Even five years ago you could not hope to capture, let alone use in a timely manner, consumer attitude and behavior patterns that could provide the kind of sustainable, profitable growth now within grasp. It was just too expensive and even counterintuitive to even attempt to attain.

The Internet and computers now provide both volume—the sheer mass of data you can look at—and the speed to use it. So the technology vector is transforming the ability both to increase understanding from this mass of data and to process and communicate it quickly to everyone in a global enterprise.

This is important because speed of learning is the only truly sustainable advantage.

We have arrived at a tipping point. The existence of all this data, plus the capabilities from a software and hardware perspective to capture, create, understand, analyze, and then communicate it internally and externally, combine to provide a new marketing mission to increase return on investment (ROI). The big news in this book comes from this convergence of new data, new ways to analyze it, new processing power, and organizations instituting the processes to link everything. The business process we propose is the link between the mass of data and the technology that provides the speed to use it.

If you are not interconnecting the collection, analysis, processing, and speedy information transmission for product development, market penetration, communications, and building brand equity, you will lose. This new capability facilitates rapid growth and has become a competitive necessity. The companies we profile in this book—Kimberly-Clark, Wachovia Bank, Microsoft, Brown-Forman, Hyatt, Gillette, and Procter & Gamble—all utilize these practices. For each company, we profile different applications of systems we recommend and include extended interviews with some of the leading industry practitioners so that you can learn from their experiences.

The problem is that not many organizations use best practices to effectively integrate their IT and marketing functions. Imagine the dialogue about this issue as companies wrestle with how to implement this change:

Management:
"We can do all this ourselves. Nothing in the technology is mysterious, nor is there anything mysterious in the organization or the process. We are a big company. We can do all this."

IT and marketing staff:
"Well, maybe. But there are external resources who know what they're doing and who have developed their systems in a much more realistic way that is much more complete than anything we have. We can probably do this, but we don't have the people, the resources, the time, etc."

So what happens? In many cases the initiative does not get done, or it is attempted in a half-baked manner and then abandoned or sidelined.

Most CEOs do not understand what they need to do. They do not commit the necessary resources, or they may see it as either a marketing project or an IT project, so it doesn't come together as a whole enterprise initiative. For example, some companies may develop a voice of the consumer website for consumer feedback, and it becomes the company "garbage can." No part of the organization owns it, it is not used properly, people have not been trained to use it, it is not interconnected, and the information thrown in is useless.

Neither marketing nor technology alone can provide this capability. We propose a companywide system with business process and technology integrated into multifunctions, with appropriate metrics, so that brands can be reignited for growth. Marketing and IT must now merge to reinvent the marketing function. This book shows you the new conceptual framework for marketing, examples of leading companies that have adopted these practices, and guidance on how to get it done.

Accordingly, we have organized this book into three parts.

Part I: "Foundation Principles and Building Blocks of the New Marketing Capability"

Chapter 1, "Open Your Mind to the New Marketing," explains how companies can increase their top-line growth.

Chapter 2, "Four Principles Supporting the New Marketing Capability," focuses on becoming customer-centric, reengineering the marketing function, rethinking the marketing organization, and redesigning technology systems.

Chapter 3, "Building Blocks of the New Marketing Capability," explores how insights and knowledge management can be utilized for innovation and product development.

Chapter 4, "Translating Insights into Innovation for Brand Financial Growth," shows how insights can be built in to the corporate culture to build customer loyalty.

Chapter 5, "Measuring Consumer Engagement," provides a new way to think about building a customer-centric process and the metrics to measure effectiveness.

Part II: "Dispatches from the Leading Edge of the New Marketing"

This part provides intimate "insider" interviews with leading marketers of major brands in major industries and companies to illustrate application and practice. The interviews and perspectives of leading executives provide real-world examples and stories of what went right and wrong in the transition to a new way to put marketing to work.

Chapter 6, "Integration of Technology and Marketing," discusses Wachovia Bank.

Chapter 7, "Open Innovation and New Product Development Through Communities of Practice," discusses Procter & Gamble's Connect and Develop strategy.

Chapter 8, "Brand Building Through Global Brand Growth," discusses Jack Daniel's®.

Chapter 9, "Growth Through Brand Portfolio and Risk Management," discusses Brown-Forman.

Chapter 10, "Insights-Led Brand Building in Technology," discusses Windows Live.

Chapter 11, "Marketing Knowledge Centers," discusses Gillette.

Chapter 12, "The New CMO," discusses Hyatt Corporation.

Part III: "How to Get It Done"

Chapter 13, "Managing Information," describes how the marketing organization can use information to become agile in applying information to real-time decision-making.

Chapter 14, "Metrics and Building the Culture of Accountability," discusses changing the corporate culture so that accountability can take hold and metrics can drive the process.

Chapter 15, "Communities of Practice for Consumer Connection and Open Innovation," describes how to partner with your consumers for continuous innovation.

Chapter 16, "Empowering Change from the Top Down," covers why the CEO must own this process and how generative, not mechanistic, change is necessary for the system to take hold and thrive.

This book is intended to help any organization harness the power of the Internet and innovative technologies. Using process and metrics to engineer the marketing function, organizations can succeed in doing the most important job to increase top-line growth—building brand equity. This is the future—and it works!

PART **I**

Foundation Principles and Building Blocks of the New Marketing Capability

1

Open Your Mind to the New Marketing

- How can the new marketing capability help companies increase their top-line growth?
- What key factors are sustaining the new marketing capabilities you need, and how do you get them?
- Can some simple principles guide your transformation to the New Marketing?

When we visit corporate executives, whatever business they are in and whatever geography they inhabit, their number one priority is always the same: "How do we generate growth, how do we sustain growth, and how do we achieve the culture of growth?" The problems of the supply side are largely solved. Supply has its processes, its software, and its metrics of efficiency. Today's focus is the demand side. The financial markets, the board of directors, and our customers all require growth. It's what matters in business today.

Growth Is Now Priority One

Survey data confirms our experience. The majority (80%) of CEOs have identified revenue growth as their primary objective. Most believe that growth will come from developing new products and entering new markets over the next five years.[1]

[1] IBM Business Consulting Services, *The Global CEO Study 2004* (IBM, 2004). Conducted with 456 CEOs.

Although the need for growth is universal, the capability for growth remains elusive. Ninety percent of those CEOs believe their companies are neither responsive enough to changing business conditions nor nimble enough to pursue new market opportunities.

Fortunately, the answer is at hand. In fact, it is right under our corporate noses. The answer is marketing.

You may recoil at this. Marketing is that slightly unsavory first cousin to sales that focuses on communications, with a little bit of glitz and a lot of spin, wrapped up in buzzwords like "positioning."

Not so. We are talking about a totally new approach to marketing—one that ignites the engines of growth and energizes the capabilities these CEOs are clamoring for. We seek to change how management, from the top down, views and implements marketing and its strategic role in their organization.

Table 1.1 summarizes the differences in our approach compared to conventional marketing.

Table 1.1   Old Versus New Marketing

Old Marketing Function	New Marketing Capability
Marketing as a cost center	Marketing as a high return on investment (ROI)
Marketing as a simplistic creative art	Marketing as a disciplined data-driven science
Marketing as unaccountable	Marketing as continuous improvement through measurable results
Marketing as high-risk	Marketing as controlled growth
Marketing as a specialized departmental function	Marketing as a core capability of growth companies
Marketing as content and creativity	Marketing as process, data, and technology

Companies with mature business units, such as Kimberly-Clark, Brown-Forman, and Wachovia, have successfully reignited their growth by developing the new marketing capability. We will show you how their marketing reengineering generated success and how you can adapt their experience to your business.

What's New: The Trends That Are Reshaping Marketing

Marketing is at the end of its old S-curve and at the beginning of the next. The S-curve, shown in Figure 1.1, is a phenomenon of advances in technology. It portrays the life of a technology that starts with a disruptive innovation, advances through competitive exploration of possibilities to achieve the breakthrough to industry standards, and then reaps its economic rewards in maturity. As it does so, the next S-curve starts to form as a new disruptive cycle begins. The new curve eventually replaces the old one.

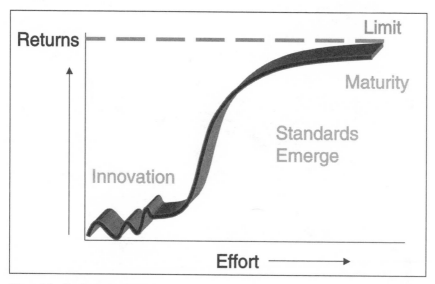

Figure 1.1 The marketing S-curve.

Marketing is on just such an S-curve. The current one is at its most extreme point—almost over. The current S-curve started in the 1930s when Proctor & Gamble (P&G) invented the market research department and the brand manager. In the 1940s and 1950s, the company added mass advertising, and then promotional marketing in the 1960s. A funnel approach was conceived, in which marketing generates as much awareness as possible to turn—by increasingly smaller percentages—that awareness into consideration, trial, repeat purchase, and loyalty. It's built-in inefficiency. That's pretty much the model that exists today. Marketing identifies customers by asking them survey questions. Advertising reaches these customers in various ways, and then Research asks them more questions to see if they "got it." Promotion offers them discounts and special offers. Management assesses the effectiveness of all this via market share (the most laggard of lagging indicators) and penetration of a mass customer base. Not only are marketing departments devoted to maintaining this model, but also the finance department that manages the budgets, and the advertising agencies and marketing services companies that spend the budgets.

That's the top of the old, aging S-curve. What's at the beginning of the new one (shown in Figure 1.2)? It has a number of key elements:

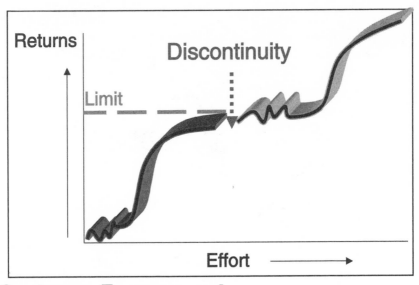

Customer Engagement

Figure 1.2   The new marketing S-curve.

- The new marketing has a different starting point. It begins with insights. An insight is a deep understanding of the motivations underlying customer behavior that can be turned directly into business action to generate new revenue. You'll see in this book how the science of generating insights has advanced, along with the process of turning insights into innovative growth initiatives.

- Insights are derived from data, and marketing now has data that couldn't be captured before. Several new methods are not only changing how data is collected; they're also generating totally new data. One example is behavioral data from the Internet. Many individual customers are now "addressable." Increasingly, marketers can reach customers individually as an electronic address that might move between a desktop computer attached to the Internet, a laptop on the go, a web-enabled mobile handheld communications device, or an iPod. Customers might be using e-mail, Instant Messenger, blogging, knowledge management tools, collaborative business software, or shopping. Marketers can reach them at most times and follow them around the web to analyze the behavior that reveals their needs.

Qualitative methods are advancing in the same direction. It is possible to conduct ethnographic studies (broadly defined as observing and recording how people behave) that generate behavioral data from around the globe. It's quite easy, via the Internet, to identify ethnographic researchers in more than 100 countries and turn them loose with a research brief. Then you quickly get data back on the behaviors of customers in each of those countries.

Electronic or behavioral, this is new data. Marketers didn't have it before; it doesn't come from surveys.

- Not only is the data new, but marketers' ability to analyze it has advanced as a result of new computational tools, both hardware-based and software-based. Statisticians and analysts can apply computational algorithms to the data to generate a totally new understanding of behavioral patterns that simply weren't available before today.

For example, Yahoo! processes 10 terabytes of data per day about consumer behavior on the Internet. Browsing patterns, shopping patterns, the relationship between information and purchase, and innumerable other behavioral data streams are available.

- Marketing can process that data more rapidly. The exponential acceleration of microprocessor capabilities and the advent of networked techniques such as distributed computing enables Yahoo! and every other marketer on the planet to generate insights from all this data. Technologies such as search engines and advanced analytics software and predictive models can troll through the data and quickly identify the patterns, anomalies, and trends. Marketers can run what-if scenarios and forecast potential outcomes with lightning speed. We have solved the needle-in-a-haystack problem. Marketing is now poised to become a genuinely data-based science.

- Marketing can share data globally with internal and external constituencies to build a new, networked capability. Via the Internet and collaborative knowledge-sharing software, we can share a greater volume of information at greater speed with more people. The result is a faster speed of learning—defined as launching an initiative into the marketplace, reading the results, and reacting with new and more effective initiative. Information sharing takes place not just within the business community of individual firms and their customers. Today, huge productivity can be mined from sharing data with a broader community of practice that has the same mission and goal but doesn't necessarily work for or do business with one company. Researchers, model-builders, academics, and peer-group panels can all participate in global data sharing and thereby accelerate the speed of learning.

- Marketing can allocate resources in new and more productive ways. The results of gathering new data, processing it with new tools and models, and sharing it in a network of global learning can include new ways to allocate resources effectively to drive growth. The new technique of resource allocation can be summarized as "Pick the winners, and advance them really fast." The winners include success models, countries that are growing quickly, new products that test well and launch well, customer groups that are becoming more loyal and generating new revenues, and new customer engagement techniques. As Larry Huston, Vice President of Innovation at Procter & Gamble, suggests, "The world is not flat; it's spiked." The new science of marketing resource allocation focuses on identifying the emerging spikes, accelerating them until they peak, and then moving on to the next set of spikes.

- Most important, marketing is learning to use process to manage the demand side with a holistic approach, in the same way that supply-side management uses process to integrate the supply chain. Think of this as an end-to-end integrated demand-management process. All of the management thinking behind the productivity revolution of the past 50 years has been centered on process as the core methodology. Yet marketing has never been a process-based discipline—until the recent advance from the old S-curve to the new one. Great advances are being made in not only mapping the processes, but also capturing them in software and making them available on every marketing practitioner's desktop across the globe. Working inside software for the first time, marketers can tap into the new data and analytics, utilize knowledge-management capabilities, and collaborate globally in open innovation networks.

The Marketing-Led Growth Model

All this adds up to a new model of marketing-led growth. New data, never before available, processed with new speed via new analytics, is shared globally with a networked internal and external marketing community. The community uses the data in a disciplined process to create new initiatives in product and service innovation, communications innovation, customer engagement innovation, and channel management innovation. Rapid introduction of the innovations to the marketplace generates some "spikes," which are identified by performance analytics and are accelerated by dynamic resource allocation. The model operates continuously to generate growth that is above the benchmark because the speed and integration of the end-to-end process capitalizes on the competitive advantage before the market can arbitrage it away. This is the new marketing.

Can you be confident in the direct link between investing in marketing—in the end-to-end capability building that encompasses insights generation, insights-into-innovation, brand building, and analytics? Subsequent chapters explore this concept in supportive detail:

- You'll read about Brown-Forman and its portfolio of brands— especially the Jack Daniel's brand. Some years ago, Chairman and CEO Owsley Brown declared that the company would invest in marketing and become the best brand builder in its industry. As a result, Brown-Forman has been able to deliver consistent revenue and profit growth. In its last annual report, sales increased 10%, and earnings grew 15% for the year, extending an impressive ten-year run of double-digit top-line and bottom-line growth. Jack Daniel's continues to be the driving force, with double-digit growth in gross profits and depletion (sales volume) growth of 8%.

- In Chapter 14, "Metrics and Building the Culture of Accountability," you will read about research conducted in the pharmaceutical industry (a particularly data-rich field). This research demonstrates the direct causal link between an increase in brand equity (defined as a measure of how customers—in this case, physicians—feel about a particular pharmaceutical brand) and a commensurate increase in market share. These increases translate directly into revenue. The model can compute the revenue value of a one-point increase in equity and the cost of a one-point increase in equity, and therefore accurately define the ROI. The model is applicable in a broad range of industries beyond pharmaceuticals.

In Chapter 5, "Measuring Consumer Engagement," you'll read about the process and metrics of customer engagement, a fundamental building block of the new marketing. This metric measures the level of customer engagement, and, in comparing one brand or company to its competitors, computes a share of customer engagement. By tracking both the cost of generating engagement and the revenue that results from it, the system delivers a measure called return on brand engagement. This is a direct measure of the ROI in marketing. Numerous case studies show returns of up to 40% (increases in revenue over increases in marketing costs). The model's validity holds in every field in which it has been applied, from automobiles to zirconia.

You can be confident in the linkage among marketing investment, the growth of brand equity (how your brand, company, product, or service is perceived by its target audience), and revenue growth and profits.

From Function to Core Capability: The Role of Marketing Redefined

The new marketing can solve the biggest challenge that CEOs face: driving and sustaining real top-line revenue growth. But doing so requires the commitment of the CEO and the management team to turn marketing into a powerful business-building tool by making it a core capability rather than a staff function.

A useful analogy is to think of marketing as a set of capital assets. If you invest in the assets appropriately, they create value and generate return. Four kinds of assets make up the marketing capability:

- Intellectual property assets are the processes, knowledge base, patents, methods, ideas, and innovations that can be shared with the customer network and marketing community. We will focus especially on the brand.
- Human assets include the talent that's inherent in the human resources recruited, cultivated, and retained; the skills that are developed through purposeful training and management; and the culture that is managed through marketing leadership.

🖋 Relationship assets include all the interactions that connect the individuals inside and outside the firm, as well as the channel and partner relationships with vendors, distributors, and service providers. It is clear that marketing will develop a new type of human capital—different people with different skills—than has been the case in the past.

🖋 Reputation assets are your external relationships with customers, channels, and partners. They are strengthened and lengthened when your reputation is good. So is your ability to recruit, retain, and leverage your human assets in your internal network. Reputation is about keeping your promises so that you develop trust. Keeping your promises requires not only intent, but investing in systems that mean that you can deliver on your marketing promises.

🖋 In addition, structural factors include the software, technology, communications, and other infrastructure to share knowledge and ideas internally; to improve intellectual property, including processes and methodologies; to bring new ideas to the market as innovation; and to help strengthen relationships with outside entities, including both customers and suppliers.

With these assets, marketing capability can be built systematically. How? By demanding the same systematization in marketing as in the corporation's other business processes. Systemization does the following:

🖋 It builds on marketing insights, business processes, and the use of technology.

🖋 It lets you measure ROI in business processes.

🖋 It enables corporations to focus investments in projects that increase ROI and shareholder value.

Marketing as a function is perceived as a staff-driven department that lies in the expenses column of the balance sheet. Marketing as a core capability is strategic and is integrated into every aspect of the organization.

Drive Top-Line Revenue Growth
by Building Brand Equity

For the 21st-century global corporation, marketing has the potential to become a driving force for shareholder value. The key asset that is leveraged for value is the brand. You will read more about brand building in subsequent chapters, but at this point, let's establish context. The term "brand" often conjures a narrow picture of familiar packaged-goods basics like Tide and Snickers. In this book, brand has a different meaning:

> A brand is that intangible capital asset that generates reliable, long-lasting, low-risk cash flows by generating loyal purchase behavior among identifiable users.

Brands that fit this definition include IBM, American Express, Cadillac, the *New York Times*, and JetBlue. You can fill in others you consider brands as well.

The breakthrough-growth company recognizes that the single most important strategic objective is to build brand equity: that set of perceptions in customers' minds associated with favorable purchase behavior and loyalty. The easiest way to understand the significance of brand equity is to recognize that brand loyalty is a function of higher brand equity. The two correlate. The cultivation of customer loyalty is the most important and easily measured objective for which marketing should be held accountable. More-consistent revenue growth, better profit margins, longer profit life cycles, and a greater likelihood of successful innovations to continue generations of long-term growth will follow.

Brand Building Is the Wisest
Investment for Sustainable Growth

Brands are assets that get stronger with time. They represent a historical accumulation of investment in the form of customer understanding, innovation, communications, distribution, public awareness and visibility, research and development (R&D), and the application of knowledge and energy by the people who have worked to support the brand over time. The longer they've been in existence, the better.

Consumers who hold strong perceptions of a brand overwhelmingly favor that brand with more frequent purchase and usage and greater loyalty (the brand fills a higher percentage of their requirements). These customers require fewer promotions and price incentives and therefore are more profitable to the corporation. They recommend the brand to their friends and coworkers and become a low-cost and highly persuasive marketing campaign on their own. They are highly receptive to brand expansion into adjacent areas of need and therefore make the introduction of new items faster, cheaper, and more profitable.

One of the great advantages of strong brands is their capacity to introduce products and services outside of a narrow category description. They can be positioned as leaders in new, innovative, emergent fields that have greater growth and profitability potential. For example, Dell is now a vast array of products, all on a single web-based customer interface and advertising platform. And the value of that brand has multiplied from when it was simply a direct-delivery desktop computer. Huggies® from Kimberly-Clark are not only diapers, but other forms of baby clothing (training pants and swimming pants), baby toiletries, and websites. They are also information exchanges to help moms answer their questions about baby development and linking them to other moms in a "community of practice" information exchange.

So, brand loyalty leads directly to higher shares, faster growth, valuable distance versus the competition, and economies of scale. These benefits translate directly into shareholder value.

This Is Not Your Father's Brand Building

You may rightly ask whether this is the same branding and positioning story we have been hearing since Rosser Reeves (*Reality in Advertising*) identified the unique selling proposition, David Ogilvy (*Confessions of an Advertising Man*) focused on a brand personality, and Trout and Ries (*Positioning*) defined positioning as the perceptual space in the consumer's mind. Indeed, if we want to go back to the 1920s, Claude Hopkins (*Scientific Advertising*) pretty much set the stage for the advertising industry in the 20th century, and others have provided variations on his theme. Their basic idea is that after the product or service is produced, it is the marketer's job to define the inherent emotional insight and/or product attribute that will create value in the consumer's mind. This assumes parity products in a category. The focus is on perception of brand value rather than a systematic integration of marketing insight, marketing management, and technology to methodically increase sustaining value for the enterprise.

The difference we propose is quite fundamental. Twentieth-century branding was focused in the customer's mind based on mass-distributed products or services advertised via mass media. Twenty-first-century marketing successes will be defined by companies that can integrate customer insights directly into a systematic application of business processes. Technology will be used to create products and services that are dynamically responsive, adaptive, and based on better and faster methods to satisfy the consumer's needs. This will happen in ways that were inconceivable in the era of mass marketing and distribution of parity products.

Growth as a Process Captured in Marketing Software

One of the most exciting aspects of the new marketing is that in the future it will be managed with the help of enterprise software systems. This development will bring all the productivity benefits of technology investments to marketing—productivity to which marketing has not had access in the past.

Marketing process can be integrated into marketing software, transforming marketing into a true business discipline.

This is the same principle that governs enterprise resource planning (ERP) software, a well-established business discipline at the "back end" of the enterprise. ERP organizes the manufacturing, logistics, and supply chain that enable the enterprise to effectively and efficiently manufacture and deliver services and products to customers and consumers.

ERP runs the supply side of virtually all corporations today. Enterprise marketing management (EMM) software will run the demand side.

It's important to understand the fundamental and revolutionary difference between ERP software and marketing software. ERP is transactional software. The steps in the process are transactions between suppliers and customers, or between internal groups and their internal customers. The software manages the transaction, focusing on matching what is "ordered" to what is "supplied."

Marketing is social software. It operates in a world of knowledge and relationships. Marketing captures data and information and processes it into insights. Then it translates those insights into innovations, communications, and experiences that build brand equity. Within the corporation, marketing is collaborative. Between the corporation and the customer, marketing builds and manages relationships. These processes are iterative, not transactional. They are flexible and responsive more than they are rules-based.

Social software is built around customer-/consumer-centric process, collaborative knowledge sharing, learning, networking, and continuous improvement via metrics.

Marketing capability incorporates the organization, skills, knowledge, technology, and resources to operate the software effectively, efficiently, and competitively.

This will not be software as we thought of it in the twentieth century— as operating systems and applications residing on laptops, desktops, and servers. This will be new software that shares knowledge and creates new knowledge through both human collaboration and continuous data loops. This software also will build intelligence by tracking customer behavior and creating the behavioral profiles that result in relevant and differentiated innovation, communication, and branded experiences. From the customer's standpoint, it is marketing "on demand"—responsive to needs and reinforcing relationships.

Figure 1.3 illustrates this end-to-end process.

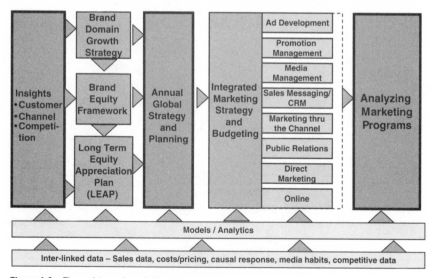

Figure 1.3 The end-to-end marketing process.

Summary

- Growth is the universal business goal.

- Growth need not be hit-or-miss or high-risk. It can be systematized and sustained.

- Marketing drives growth when it is viewed as a capability rather than a specialized function.

- The elements of capability are process, knowledge sharing, innovation skills and execution, relationship building and learning, and responding through measurement. Technology captures and systematizes this capability.

- The equivalent technology for the supply side is ERP—transactional management software.

- The software for demand creation and demand management is social software rather than transactional software.

- This social software can be systematically structured using component business modeling and can be made available on demand.

2

Four Principles Supporting the New Marketing Capability

▸ How does the enterprise integrate best practices into all areas of marketing?

▸ How can technology leverage the marketing system?

▸ How can customers become the drivers of marketing, not the target?

▸ What is the difference between enterprise marketing solutions and point solutions, and why does it matter?

We stated at the end of the last chapter that marketing capability incorporates the organization, skills, knowledge, technology, and resources to operate social software effectively, efficiently, and competitively.

A company that embraces this statement must transform itself to realize the growth promise inherent in it. In other words, it must "operationalize" the capability. By operationalize, we mean it is necessary to go one step further toward understanding the idea that "marketing is software." When you think conventionally, you separate the ideas of marketing and technology in your head. You might think that marketing is a function and that it can be supported by technology—such as e-mail or online customer research or online advertising or ERP-based budgeting tools. Or you might think in organizational terms and envision the marketing and IT departments as two distinct boxes on the organization chart.

But you must dismiss both thoughts from your mind, along with any other thoughts that marketing and technology are somehow separate. Marketing and IT must be strategically and structurally inseparable to make the changes necessary to achieve sustained top-line revenue growth.

We propose that the marketing function become a business process system driven by technology to enhance brand equity.

Marketing integrates knowledge, intelligence, and interpretation. You develop knowledge of your customers, use the intelligence you have developed over time to process that knowledge, and then implement the interpretation in strategy, innovation, communications, and delivery of the brand experience. Implementation creates new knowledge that updates the intelligence and drives the system to continuous improvement. Technology must be the oxygen for this living system. It must be the fuel for the engine.

It's hard to think like this. So let's start from an easier place, with some principles that can support this new marketing capability (see Table 2.1).

Table 2.1 Four Steps to Marketing Transformation

Principle	Description
Reorient so that customers are the drivers of marketing, not the target	The most critical point of view—the one that really matters—is the customer's; the customer has the power.
Reengineer your marketing processes	Process is designed to deliver value to the customer; extraneous activity is eliminated.
Rethink your marketing organization	Replace functional specialization with cross-company collaborative customer value creation.
Redesign your marketing technology	Marketing is an enterprise system rather than a series of point solutions.

This chapter explains these foundation principles. Part II, "Dispatches from the Leading Edge of the New Marketing," of this book illustrates these principles through case studies.

Reorient So That Customers Are the Drivers of Marketing, Not the Target

The new marketing requires a different attitude toward the customer. The customer becomes the organization's partner, and the organization adapts and responds based on continuous listening and learning from customers.

This attitude is critical to adopt because the customer is now in control. Chapter 5, "Measuring Consumer Engagement," considers the new rules of engaging with customers through communications in the digital age. You'll see how customers control what messages they receive and the media via which they receive them, as well as how this completely changes the methods of managing communications and measuring their effectiveness. Chapter 12, "The New CMO," gives you an insider's view of how technology and marketing have merged in the hospitality industry. You'll see how customers directly drive hotel operations through online reservations systems and preferences management.

This new age of customers in control requires a reversal of the marketing flow.

Organizations that practice the new marketing are characterized by their ability to rapidly and continuously sense, interpret, decide, and act on information from customers. They sense what is truly valuable to their customers and then respond in turn with a value proposition developed around customers' individual requirements. Although this concept represents a dramatic departure from conventional marketing strategies, it is emerging as a new imperative in a world where customers will continue to have more choices and more control. IBM calls it "Adaptive Marketing," so let's use that term.

Because it is impossible to predict what customers will do, adaptive marketers don't even try. Conventional research techniques ask questions through surveys or focus groups and try to predict what consumers will do by analyzing their responses. In Adaptive Marketing, the reverse approach applies: research observes or measures what customers do and deduces their motivations. From the data, marketers derive insights as to what drives the observed behavior and then utilize the insight to drive innovations and design customer experiences that encourage reinforcement of positive customer behaviors or changes in negative customer behaviors. The "make it and then market it" approach can give customers the impression that you don't really know or care who they are or what they want. In contrast, adaptive marketers opt to employ the "sense and respond" strategy. This allows customers to tell marketers— through their behavior—who they are, what they value, what they want, and how they want it.[1]

[1] IBM Business Consulting Services, *Adaptive Marketing: Building an intuitive enterprise* (IBM, 2003).

Becoming adaptive begins with an executive commitment to the principles of Adaptive Marketing, based on the following beliefs:

- The most critical point of view—the one that really matters—is the customer's; the customer holds the power.
- The only viable strategy in a constantly changing world centers around being adaptive.
- Communications with customers are driven by individual customer profiles.
- Contact points, regardless of the channel, should be designed with the total customer experience in mind.
- Service operations should become adaptive so that the enterprise can effectively respond to customer requests.

The lasting return on this investment is clear and simple to achieve: a greater ability to sense and respond to the needs of your customer; a more satisfied, more loyal customer base; and a business designed to thrive.

The Community of Customers

A good example of adapting to customers in a way that can only be achieved via technology—and that, in fact, *is* technology—is facilitating customer communities via the Internet. The brand owner can initiate such a community but exercises no control and succeeds only by adapting to the community dynamic. The community will grow organically to build and exchange knowledge and to develop members' capabilities. Members are self-selecting, and they join and exit at will. Passion, commitment, and identification with the group's experience are the only qualifications for entry and participation. The community keeps going so long as members are interested in maintaining the group.

A simple example is the Huggies® Baby Network. It's a community of first-time moms who get together electronically to share information and knowledge about bringing up baby—"child development" would be the official term. Huggies brand encourages this community. It aims to serve a group of moms who believe that their own instincts about bringing up baby are preferable to the more prescriptive approaches of some competitive brands and of elitist "baby experts." Moms are the real baby experts. Huggies wants to give them a forum to share their expertise, gain more knowledge, and develop more independent capabilities through knowledge sharing.

Huggies employs Yahoo!'s technology and platform as one of the access points to the Baby Network. Yahoo! is another example of a brand that is strengthened by its encouragement of the creation of independent customer communities. Whether it's fantasy football or singles online dating services, the powerful marketing concept of communities of customers is one that Yahoo! has harnessed effectively for the benefits of both its users and advertisers.

Table 2.2 offers a snapshot of communities of customers.

Table 2.2 Snapshot: Communities of Customers

Question	Answer
What's the community's purpose?	To develop members' capabilities to build and exchange knowledge
Who belongs?	Members who select themselves
What holds it together?	Passion, commitment, and identification with the group's expertise
How long does it last?	As long as there is interest in maintaining the group

Marketing Instrumentation in Software

Another example of the adaptive function at work is marketing instrumentation embedded in software. Essentially, this technology enables the software to talk to the customer and to send back to the brand owner the data that reports on customer behavior. Outbound instrumentation can do a lot of the job of marketing communications, such as telling the user when a new feature has been automatically added via Internet-enabled upgrading, or suggesting usage enhancements based on the user's behavior. Inbound instrumentation can build behavioral profiles of the user, such as which features she uses most and how many people she collaborates with. In turn, this information can be used to customize new solutions.

In all of these examples—customer behavior research driving innovation, customer communities on the web, instrumentation in software—the customer is in control and the marketer responds and adapts to the customer's behavior.

Reengineer Your Marketing Processes

Marketing has never been viewed as a process-based discipline. In fact, quite the opposite is the case. The culture of marketing is often one of "leave me alone" creativity. Just leave the ad agency alone, and it will come up with a great campaign. Just leave the sales promotion team alone, and they'll come up with something to boost fourth-quarter sales. Marketing has often been cast as the owner of the "silver bullet" that will solve the marketplace's problems with a flash of inspiration.

In the new marketing world, the opposite approach will bring more sustainable and reliable success. The productivity advances that have been made in supply-chain systems over the past 30 years began with process mapping (a methodical visual depiction of the decisions and actions required for any project). As soon as a "process map" is in place, you can identify where variances and inconsistencies exist, where time can be speeded up, where cost can be taken out, and where value can be shifted. People can be trained in the process and can work more efficiently when they have clear knowledge of each other's roles and responsibilities. Technology can be brought to bear to automate parts of a mapped process, freeing the human factor for more-productive value-added tasks. Without process, none of this productivity advance can take place.

In business, the definition of process is a series of steps and activities that transform an input into an output that has value for a customer. It would be hard to find a more succinct definition of marketing. The input is customer behavior, translated into knowledge and customer understanding. The output is a customer benefit that might be delivered in a product, service, or relationship. The value is measured by the person's loyalty and value as a customer. The process equation is clear in marketing. The challenge is to map it; codify it; and provide the marketers and their ecosystem with a process-based system that they can use, measure, and improve.

There are precedents for such a process-based system. Diageo, when it was still a conglomerate with business in alcoholic beverages and food, developed a system called the Diageo Way of Brand Building, which was known affectionately inside the company as DWEEB. The system was an effort to codify a methodology for building brand value, whether that brand was in the whiskey category or the baking category. DWEEB distilled the company's intellectual property in marketing into series of linked tools and methodologies. The tools were processes and models for transforming knowledge, information, and data about the consumer (the inputs) into brand innovation, consumer experience design, and brand communications, the three major resources for brand value creation.

The system was published in a series of booklets and also was delivered via training and presentations. This was an appropriate knowledge-sharing approach in the days before it was understood how technology could support a knowledge-based process. Surprisingly, there have not been a lot of advances since DWEEB.

Cisco has developed an example that is a bit more attuned to the Internet world. During the 1990s, Cisco acquired many companies to add to the suite of capabilities it offered customers in the Internet/networking space. The Cisco brand name was very strong, and it was important to the value-creation model that Cisco presented a single-branded solution in a complex field where customers were anxiously seeking reassurance and reliability. Therefore, Cisco developed an Internet-based marketing knowledge, process, and operations center that all newly acquired companies could access to get information and develop an understanding of the Cisco way of going to market. Processes, methodologies, tools, templates, and examples were all available, from how to develop a marketing plan and marketing budget and get them approved to how to use approved logos and content in a product sell sheet. New Cisco employees could become Cisco-trained and Cisco-supported marketers instantly.

Process Discipline Unleashes Creativity

With defined processes, creativity can be directed toward improving measured performance and can be objectively evaluated. Innovation can occur only in context, and process provides the context and the opportunity for marketing excellence, as we illustrate in Part II with our case studies.

End-to-end process involves every aspect of a brand, from initial concept through production, distribution, and continuous innovation. These are the benefits for end-to-end process adoption in marketing:

- **Best practice:** Marketing managers can share and standardize the achievement of a particular function, such as great point-of-sale practices for packaged goods in a retail channel. The current best practice will be captured and adopted with continuous learning through a shared community of practice among marketing professionals across brands.

- **Springboard from which to leap higher:** Having codified best practices as you know them, you have constructed a springboard from which to leap even higher. Marketing practitioners throughout the company, who view and use the process, will volunteer improvements in output quality, speed, and cost.

- **Viral:** As soon as you begin enhancing one process, you are driven to improve the whole marketing process, from end to end and top to bottom. An example might be the realization that, when the brand equity management process is codified, it can be enhanced via the codification of an insights process as an input.

- **Generates measurable improvement and return on marketing investment (ROMI):** Sound process management requires standards. The process enhancers in both this and the next marketing generation will learn how to share excellence across a common platform. Although many principles must be applied to ascertain whether improvements are genuine, the best one is performance measurement: Is the output better? ROMI can be tracked only if outputs and inputs are measured. Measurement can be linked to the relevant activity that produced it only if a process exists to join inputs to outputs.

- **Knowledge and training:** Marketers want on-the-job training they can apply immediately. A well-conceived process that is fully developed and generously presented constitutes some of the best training a corporation can offer. The process, having been distilled from years of experience and the learning that comes from repeated use, represents the corporation's accumulated knowledge and its experts in the area where the process applies.

P&G is one company that has brought the liberating discipline of process to marketing, with outstanding results. Its simple but effective approach is typified by its marketing return on investment (ROI) process:

- Each of the many thousands of marketing initiatives implemented around the world each year is documented in a "booklet." The booklet sets a target for the initiative's financial outcome, expressed as total revenue generated minus the costs of doing so, netted to today's value via a Net Present Value (NPV) calculation.

- Each initiative is evaluated by comparing the actual NPV to the target NPV.

- When this process was initiated, only 20% of initiatives made their NPV target and the total NPV delivery was less than 80% of goal.
- After several years, 80% of initiatives made their NPV target, and total NPV delivery is more than 120%.
- P&G simply divides its initiatives into terciles (three categories). The top third are initiatives that work really well. The bottom third are those that miss badly. To get outstanding results, the company simply stops using initiatives that fall in the bottom tercile and begins using more of those that fall in the top tercile.

Voila! It's a process. It's not rocket science. And it doesn't require that you achieve some not-very-useful precision in calculating an ROI number. It simply requires that you divide the effectiveness of your marketing initiative results into terciles: what worked, what didn't, and those in the middle.

And it unleashes creativity by focusing ideation on further developing the initiative types that have worked well in the past.

Rethink Your Marketing Organization

Marketing must not be a functional silo in a rigid organizational structure. It must be a capability that infuses the organization with adaptive customer-centricity.

As soon as processes are in place, organizational thinking, rewards systems, and people systems need to be aligned.

The major organizational change in thinking is to emphasize lateral collaboration around process rather than departmental hierarchies of structure. Marketing is a lateral function. Data about customer behavior flows in from the "front end" of the engagement with the customer— from the sales force, customer management teams, website, retail point-of-sale data, and so on. The data is turned into insights. The insights are transformed into new products, services, or solutions that meet the identified needs of the customers expressed in the insights. And then the front end of the company presents the solution to the customer and measures the acceptance, attitude changes, behavior changes, and revenue and profit effects. This is a two-way lateral work flow. There is no way it can be achieved by a hierarchical structure in which different groups find barriers to sharing information or collaborating around insights.

Marketing organizations must be defined by the processes for creating customer value and the work flows that underpin them. Roles and responsibilities must be assigned based on the right skills and information to complete the process step and hand off to the next one. The marketing transformation will make the hierarchical organization chart obsolete and replace it with the process map and its associated roles and responsibilities.

Who will you hire to provide the human capital for this high-performance system? In the past, marketing "types" were creative ideators who had the inspiration to come up with great sales and marketing campaigns or develop great graphical communications. Tomorrow's breakthrough marketing requires a different hiring mind-set:

- **Strong business orientation:** The goal of marketing is to drive profitable growth, and that must be the marketer's mind-set.
- **Strong technology bent:** Marketing is software, and you need people to operate it who are technology enthusiasts.
- **Strong collaborators:** The old marketing mind-set was sometimes characterized more by individual creativity than collaborative development. But this is less useful—and potentially destructive— in the new operating environment.

Redesign Your Marketing Technology: Enterprise Systems Rather Than Point Solutions

Say the words "marketing technology" to most IT professionals, and they immediately think of point solutions—technology that does one thing well. That "point solution" might be an e-mail engine for outbound e-mail campaigns or a market mix modeling tool for analyzing the relative effectiveness of different marketing expenditures and vehicles. Your marketing department is probably accumulating many of these tools or using them via specialist suppliers.

We believe that you should have in mind a much more expansive technology-supported marketing capability.

Customer-facing technology must put the customer in control. There must be a direct linkage from the customer making a choice or stating a preference to your company's back-end operations that is suitably enabled to respond. Tom O'Toole of Hyatt Corporation explains this concept in Chapter 12.

Internally, marketing technology should consistently deliver best practices and business processes to everyone in the corporation—24/7. You should seek to enable them to use the processes to effectively execute marketing initiatives and measure their success. You should aim to knit together everybody in the horizontal, collaborative marketing work flow to jointly accomplish a full range of marketing work process requirements:

- Create common process standards and the ability to work over a diverse network at high speeds. Everyone can be working off a common set of data, simultaneously or asynchronously, that can be instantly arrayed and conveyed.

- Provide a common language for understanding, progressing, and revising projects that can be worked on immediately and changed quickly as required.

- Reduce wasted time by increasing standardization where appropriate—freeing time for creativity.

- Bring new people on a team up a steep learning curve very quickly, because the training is inherent when people work with the digital content and in the process.

- Expedite approvals. Doing so can provide the work to be reviewed and approved, circulate it automatically, aggregate comments and suggestions, and alert managers to the process of approvals through the chain.

Enterprise Marketing Systems Versus Point Solutions

Most organizations have used only very basic technology tools to support their marketing operations. Most of these solutions have been either homegrown or developed using third-party providers of point solutions (intended for limited use for a particular marketing task, such as customer data files). The traditional suppliers to the marketing process, such as prepress houses and media agencies, have created licensed or hosted applications to help automate processes in their own domain. However, these technologies have been designed to address only part of one process or, at best, only one process. They are not scalable and are not integrated to meet the end-to-end needs of all the marketing processes and do not provide the required content. In fact, one reason why many efforts to institute customer relationship management (CRM) failed is because there was no mapping of the associated process, and no content support. CRM's fatal flaw is that it records interactions with consumers but is unable to enhance the interaction using knowledge, or to interpret the interaction and make it better.

In the absence of an integrated solution, many of the homegrown and third-party applications are eagerly adopted. However, significant gaps exist in the current IT support for marketing:

- **End-to-end coverage:** The current applications are disparate point solutions and do not support end-to-end processes and content.
- **Ad hoc development:** Isolated development has led to point solutions that do not integrate with each other. The consequences include data redundancy, manual entry and reentry, usability issues in doing work in different places, maintenance issues, and a plethora of additional issues that are typical of a fragmented approach to development for a functional area.
- **Duplicated functionality:** Many applications have components and infrastructure elements that are duplicated but implemented differently.
- **Nonstandard data:** Various examples of inconsistencies in data (such as different product hierarchies used by sales and marketing) lead to problems in integrating marketing with the enterprise application infrastructure.
- **Data integration with external data providers:** This is a major problem given the issues of dissimilar product hierarchy, accounting for special deals, and other such data integration issues.

These gaps in existing technology for marketing process support are significant. However, this should not be an obstacle for the chief marketing officer (CMO) to achieve his or her ultimate goal of building brand equity. This list summarizes the end-to-end technology we advocate to reengineer marketing to become a business core competency:

- It meets the effectiveness and efficiency requirements of end-to-end business processes. The technology can ultimately meet the functional requirements of all elements of marketing within one solution.
- It uses a single integrated system that consolidates the current use of disparate information silos.
- It has an easily configurable user interface that can provide different interfaces for different constituents. It also supports multiple end-user operating system platforms, content viewers, and web browsers.
- It offers easy standards-based integration with added tools within the solution set, as well as other enterprise applications.
- It leverages existing IT application platform standards and investments for both current and planned enterprise software purchases. It also utilizes in-place procurement and vendor relationships to the fullest extent possible to limit costs.
- It is cost-effective to improve company profit margins, ROI, total cost of ownership (TCO), and long-term maintenance costs.

The Importance of Content in Enterprise Marketing Management Systems

Many marketers in large global organizations are accustomed to ad hoc and personal styles. So it is a great challenge to introduce new processes. Both the content and its structure are very important to the adoption of new processes. The content should be structured in a way that makes it easily accessible and applicable during the execution of the process. Content in the form of digital templates, checklists, scorecards, and tips is "user-friendly" for ready application in a day-to-day work environment, as opposed to the tomes of training manuals lying long forgotten on the shelf.

Best-practices content can be instantly delivered to the users. We call this just-in-time (JIT) expertise. This enables the relevant knowledge and best practices to be pushed to a particular user as they are doing a task. This push mechanism dramatically increases the likelihood of content usage during work.

Summary

◢ Marketing processes should drive the use of IT to address the most important priorities for growth in your enterprise.

◢ The marketing organization should be changed so it is less departmental and more cross-functional. The adoption of business practices based on technology for brand building should be "job one."

◢ Marketing should become adaptive to your customers. Learn from customer behavior, and interpret it via insights to design and deliver products and services that enhance customer experiences.

◢ IT should be an "end-to-end" integrated system so that it is easy to integrate into all facets of the job, rather than being a specific point solution.

3

Building Blocks of the New Marketing Capability

- Are you generating true, valuable insights?
- Are you generating insights that are good for innovation?
- How do you make insights generation a systemic capability?
- Are you fully utilizing the experience and creativity of every function to generate insights for innovation?
- How do you apply insights to create successful innovations?
- What's your speed of innovation, and how does it compare to that of the competition?
- What factors can you track and measure to monitor innovation?

The new marketing model is focused on driving growth. This capability has two basic building blocks: innovation and delivering that innovation to customers via branded solutions and experiences. This chapter touches on how marketing fuels innovation by generating insights. The next chapter discusses how to deliver innovation.

What Is an Insight, and Why Is It Important?

Innovation should be the primary engine of growth. Two of the most powerful words in the marketing lexicon are "different" and "better." Those are customer-centric words. The customer is searching for solutions that are different and better. The companies that deliver on the needs for "different and better" are the ones with loyal customers and consistent top-line revenue growth.

How can you drive innovation? Where does it come from? Our contention is that it is both engendered and delivered by the marketing process. Marketing bestrides the field of innovation like a colossus. The first footprint is the *input* to the innovation process, which we call insights. The second footprint is the *output* of the innovation process, which is the brand experience.

We define an insight as a profound understanding of the customer and customer needs that explains their behavior (or non-behavior) and that can be turned into a profitable business idea.

Note the focusing idea of *explaining behavior*. Marketing should accurately tap consumer attitudes to provide the right goods and services. Then it can use scientific practices to influence consumer attitudes to change behavior. The behavior we seek to affect is the economic one of purchasing, loyalty, and increasing share of requirements. That can come only as a result of changing attitudes. This insight is critical because it sheds light on the motivations that drive behavior, and therefore on what we must do to change behavior.

Insights build and sustain winning brands. They create advantage across the entire brand-building continuum, from the moment of truth contained in the core insight, to the moment of truth across the buyer's desk, to the in-use moment of truth when the customer experiences the product or service.

Moments of Truth

Every marketing team can win an increased share of the customer's heart by developing insights that allow the brand to own the "moment of truth." The three moments of truth are as follows:

- **The core of your brand promise:** For Nike that seminal moment of truth is not about shoes; it's about "self-realization through exercise." It's about Nike owning that feeling you get not from winning a race but from doing your best. To its millions of adherents, the Nike swoosh is a talismanic symbol that "I care about doing my very best."

● **Just before the purchase, when the buyer is considering an array of choices:** This is the moment of truth at the shelf, where the customer passes judgment on the array of benefits, both real and emotional, you are offering her. For virtually all consumer packaged-goods brands, this has been the most neglected consumer touch point.

● **The product in use and the combination of "brand touches" during that usage experience reinforce the customer's loyalty to the brand:** Apple's iPod in-use moment of truth combines the ease of downloading (and paying with your credit card!), the simplicity of using the iPod's software functions and interface, and the sensuousness of the design. No matter what your product or service, no matter whether your buyer is a 12-year-old girl using her iPod or a power shovel operator using your equipment, you must deliver an in-use moment of truth experience that is defined by the user. Table 3.1 elaborates.

Table 3.1 The Apple iPod Fulfills the Need for Unique Self-Expression

Moment of Truth	Description
Core insight moment of truth	Apple users are motivated by an intense need for self-expression. This need can be met not only in the desktop computer hardware and software business, but also in the digital content (music and video) users store, manipulate, and consume.
Purchase moment of truth	iPod purchasers pursue choice and options and will pay a premium for greater control. For example, in an iPod Shuffle, the software controls the order of play. But in a premium iPod, the user controls the order of play, for which he or she gladly spends more money. The user also pays a premium for design and color options and personalization such as engraving the case.
Usage moment of truth	The user experience is complemented by two things. iTunes is the online software that allows users to download the songs they want. The iPod resident software enables users to control the play order and the content. Therefore, the users' iPod experience is totally controlled by them, and their iPod experience is truly and uniquely individual.

Insights Generation as a Process

Insights generation is a core competency of the innovative company. That's why you should build a process and develop a best-practices organizational construct and a range of tools to turn your company into an insights-hungry, insights-discovery machine.

Process means transforming an input into an output that's of use to the customer. In our case, we've defined the output of the insights process as innovation and the brand experience.

The starting input is data and information (see Figure 3.1). Chances are, you have enough data and information; if not, you can easily get it. The first challenge is to turn the data into knowledge and to make that knowledge easily accessible and shared across the entire organization. We'll discuss this issue more in Chapter 10, "Insights-Led Brand Building in Technology." But knowledge is not insight. We can know something without understanding its implications. Insights generation is the establishment of a shared understanding of what drives customer behavior. This includes sufficient utility for us to reinforce that behavior (if it is favorable to us), to expand that behavior to get the customer to buy more, or to change that behavior by getting the customer to switch from the competition and/or to buy our new product or service.

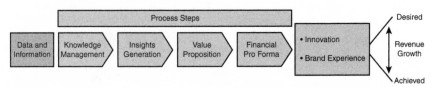

Figure 3.1   The insights process.

Let's explore a couple of these concepts briefly.

Knowledge Management

The Voice of the Customer

One of the ways the customer-centric organization prevents any erosion of the customer-centric viewpoint is to structure its knowledge management around the voice of the customer. This is a simple concept:

Any data that comes into the corporation from any field is further processed to represent knowledge of the customers—their behavior, attitudes, preferences, trends, and attributes. Chapter 10 provides details about the voice of the customer as a knowledge management tool. The emphasis here is that insights generation starts with customer data that is organized and accessible so that everyone in the organization can locate, view, and cross-compare the latest data about customers, consumers, channels, and competitors.

Learning Plan

The second critical element of knowledge management for the insights generation process is the learning plan. Any data user can examine the voice-of-the-customer data and identify gaps—knowledge that the company doesn't have but needs. The user then submits a learning request. These learning requests are rolled up and prioritized. The prioritization might be at the business unit level, the brand level, the country level, or the enterprise level, depending on the corporation's growth priorities. The corporation decides how much it wants to invest in learning this year, and the priority learning requests are fulfilled to the extent that the budget permits.

New learning is added to the voice of the customer and is circulated to subscribers so that they always have the most recent knowledge. As you will see in the steps of using value propositions and the corresponding financial pro forma, companies can make progress toward identifying a return on knowledge that will further refine their learning investment strategy.

Insights-Generation Tools

Insights don't come directly from data and analytics. They require what some technologists refer to dismissively as "wetware"—human intervention. On the other hand, insights generation need not be feared as an inspirational "aha" moment that arrives only unpredictably via vintage-champagne-fueled musings of the super-creative guru. Wetware is not quite that wet.

In fact, we have proven that insights generation can become a predictable, measurable, repeatable capability of the well-motivated and well-equipped team. Our tools of preference for this capability are the insights workshop and the "six connects."

The insights workshop uses multiple principles of human dynamics. The first principle is that it's best to work via a cross-functional team representing multiple perspectives and expertise, using collaboration and accelerated interactive techniques to quickly generate, sort, and prioritize ideas. Another principle is that the best process involves small teams working together to generate ideas from one perspective. Then the teams come together in a large group to share those ideas and arrive at the next-generation synthesis. In turn, they go back to a small-team exercise, come back together in a large team to share and synthesize, and so on until one or two emerging "super solutions" are generated. Using this and other tools, our insights workshops have generated insights that consistently lead to profitable innovation.

The "six connects" tool is a good example of unleashing human creativity through technological enablement. This tool can easily be provided via an insights-generation software module and can be automated to some extent. The six connects are as follows:

- Connect behavior to needs and emotions. Examples: Dove, iPod.
- Connect to consumer hopes and fears. Examples: Botox, Michelin.
- Connect heavy-usage data to emotional brand loyalty. Example: Gillette.
- Connect to insights used by others also targeting your consumer segment. Example: Coach benchmarking with spa marketers.
- Connect to experts. Examples: sociologists, anthropologists, psychologists, and market analysts.
- Connect to long-term trends. Examples: demographic changes, broad lifestyle changes, category trends, technology changes.

The "six connects" exercises start with the question "What behavior (or non-behavior) do I want to explain?" and conclude with an insights statement such as the following:

The target group behaves in fashion X because of motivation Y. The opportunity to change/modify/enhance this behavior is Z.

An example is a target group of women who consider undergoing plastic surgery (see Figures 3.2 and 3.3). Their motivation is that, as they get older, they believe that their attractiveness is impaired by the effects of aging. The consequence is that they feel a loss of self-esteem. To recover their attractiveness and self-esteem, they believe that an expert technological intervention is required. This opportunity is defined by the facts that this feeling is widely held and that the solution is limited by both its expense and risk. The delivery of a less-expensive but still-credible solution could create a new value stream among a much broader target group.

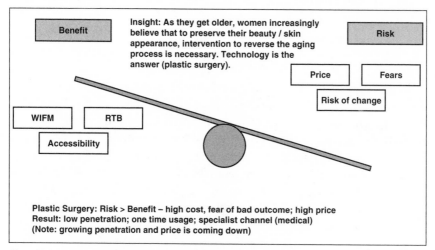

Figure 3.2   How insights rebalance the value proposition: before.
Note: WIFM=What's In It For Me?

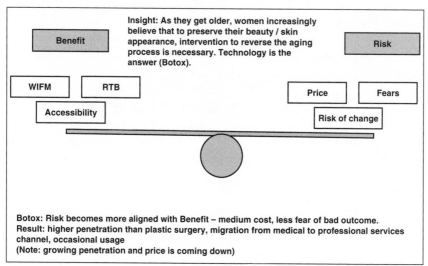

Figure 3.3   How insights rebalance the value proposition: after.
Note: WIFM=What's In It For Me?

This insight has generated several value streams. Botox is one example. It's technological, less expensive than plastic surgery, and more easily available through dermatologists and estheticians rather than surgeons. Olay is another. It's technological (that's why Olay marketers use names like "Regenerist" in describing their formula), it's less expensive than Botox, and it's available at your local drugstore. Olay revenue has grown 2,000% in the last 15 years.

Value Proposition

How do we know the insight will create value? We must attach it to a value proposition. Few value propositions are new. Most rebalance an existing value proposition and make it available to more users or enable more-frequent usage. The value proposition for plastic surgery comes from the same insight as the value proposition for Botox, but the Botox brand makes the solution more available to more women, who feel the same way as the surgery-users. When the perceived risk is lowered (both price and in-use risk), the same benefits become available to a broader audience.

Financial Pro Forma

From the value proposition, it's an easy step to the financial pro forma. How much revenue will this insight and its associated value proposition generate, and how much will it cost to commercialize? The downstream revenues can be estimated by identifying the number of users and the price per use. The calculation can be validated in various ways—through modeling, surveys, research, and concept testing. How accurate are these estimates? At first, they will not be very accurate. But the act of making them can then generate a measurement tool (how close were we?), and the requisite skills and algorithms can be refined over time. You'll develop valuable intellectual property in the modeling and estimation of insights-based pro formas, which generates value in and of itself.

Summary

- Everyone in the organization can generate and refine insights methodically.
- Insights can be transformed into innovation through business processes.
- Consumers can partner with the organization to improve product development.
- "Six connects" can unleash human creativity through process and technology.
- Innovation factors can serve as guidelines for transforming your organization.

4

Translating Insights into Innovation for Brand Financial Growth

🖋 How is innovation guided by insights in a marketing-led process?

🖋 How does innovation turn an insight into a revenue- and profit-generating business action?

🖋 What new people skills are required to lead the insights-into-innovation process?

🖋 How do you make Discover, Design, and Deliver the cornerstones of your innovation system?

Insights are the raw material for innovation. If you have identified an insight about your customers' needs, it's possible that you can meet those needs in a unique and superior way. You've created a growth opportunity. The next step in the process is to turn that opportunity into revenue by identifying, designing, and delivering the innovation to the marketplace.

Innovation in some companies is often seen as hit-or-miss. However, it need not be so. There are three preventable causes of the risks with innovation (the chance that the innovation will not meet its marketplace goals):

🖋 The innovation is not based on a true insight.

🖋 Innovation is not managed as a process that can be engineered, measured, and continuously improved.

🖋 Creativity is not integrated into the process. "Stages and gates" interfere with "design to delight."

Chapter 3, "Building Blocks of the New Marketing Capability," explained the insights-generation component of the innovation process. This chapter focuses on the insights-into-innovation component. These processes are illustrated in Part II, "Dispatches from the Leading Edge of the New Marketing," with the case studies and perspectives from industry leaders.

Even though innovation is a business process, as responsive to process design and engineering as any other, it is not the same as other business processes. Innovation is often treated as a supply-side process, centered around producing new products and services, the required technology, and the appropriate resource supply chain. In this view, the innovation process is built on competencies in engineering, technology, R&D, and procurement.

If you take the view that innovation is a *demand-side* process—centered around customers and their needs, the competencies and the process design change dramatically. The innovation task is a marketing task in the sense that we redefine marketing in this book to identify and understand customer needs and to translate the need-state data into innovative solutions that customers will buy. The first step in managing demand generation for predictable success is to think about innovation as a demand-side process.

Table 4.1 summarizes this difference.

Table 4.1 Comparison of the Supply-Side and Demand-Side Innovation Processes

Innovation as a Supply-Side Process	Innovation as a Marketing (Demand-Side) Process
Product-centric	Customer-centric
Leverages technology	Leverages customer knowledge and insight
Driven by engineering, technology, and R&D competencies	Driven by competencies in identifying and meeting customer needs
Objective: bringing effective new products and services to market	Objective: building growing brands and businesses through innovative solutions for customers
Goal: new/superior product features that outperform the competition	Goal: new/elevated emotional benefits that generate more loyal customer behavior
Measure: side-by-side performance comparisons	Measure: customer attitudes
The "old" marketing role is at the end of the process, adding communications prior to launch	The "new" marketing role is from the beginning to the end of the process by bringing and maintaining customer-centric focus

The right people to lead this process are marketers. Not the classically trained "old" marketers with expertise in positioning and communication, but the "new" marketers. The new marketer combines a high level of technical competence with a high level of sensitivity to consumer and customer emotional needs. Without technical competency, it is impossible to manage the insights-into-innovation process. With the combination of technical competency and emotional sensitivity, the new marketers are uniquely qualified to manage the process's special characteristics:

- They have expertise in taking relatively "soft" or qualitative data such as customer attitudes and needs and combining this data with more quantitative inputs (such as trends in purchase data). They are not deterred by "soft" data the way engineers might be.

- They bring analytical decision support tools to sort through the combination of hard and soft data to develop an understanding of the optimal directions for innovation. For example, a standard Brand Equity Monitor tracks the cause-and-effect linkage between brand equity scores ("soft" data) and financial outcomes ("hard" data). It can isolate the relative effect of different kinds of innovations and identify which ones have the greatest effect on revenues and profits.

- They use collaboration tools to translate their understanding into instructions for collaborative resources to follow. In the communications field, an example of such a tool at work is the Communications Brief. It's an instruction set for creative resources (such as advertising agencies, designers, website builders, and event managers) to follow. It sets out the precise details of the target audience, the emotional and functional benefits to be communicated, the support data for the claims that the brand can deliver the benefit, and even the tone and manner and character guidelines for the communications. The creative agencies are free to be creative within the guidelines, and the marketers can use the Communications Brief to judge the creative submissions. The same can be done with an Innovation Brief. It helps the technologists identify the benefits customers seek and the features that will deliver the benefits. The technologists can quickly achieve a contextual focus on what to produce and the designers what to design using the same guidelines of target audience, benefits, and style.

- They are comfortable with using creativity tools to generate big, disruptive ideas and lots of them. Marketers are not deterred by the process of going from a broad "top of the funnel" (lots of as-yet-unproven creative ideas) to a narrow, focused, measurable "end of the funnel" (one big idea of proven potential).

- They are skilled in the use of testing tools that can ascertain the effect of innovation on customer attitudes and the models to project these attitudes into revenue-generating purchase behavior.

- They have command of the delivery-to-market tools based on the success models they create by measuring the success of different introductory campaigns and promotions for new innovations and solutions.

Figure 4.1 shows an effective market-driven innovation process.

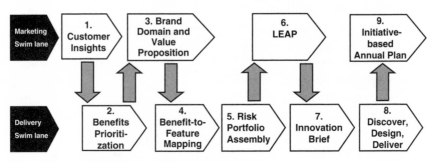

Figure 4.1   The market-driven innovation process.

Process mapping experts call the horizontal rows in which the steps are arranged "swim lanes." Swim lanes are allocated to functions, and then collaborative activities that involve multiple functions are identified by the linking arrows that cross the swim lanes. We'll call the two swim lanes in this process map the marketing swim lane and the delivery swim lane. The marketing swim lane is led by the experts in understanding customers and their needs and in building brands via strong and resilient emotional bonds with customers. The delivery swim lane is led by the technologists, engineers, technicians, R&D teams, designers, and procurement experts who can ensure that the targeted innovation can be operationalized and brought to market. The team members work together from the outset and in every step in each swim lane. This way, the technologists, engineers, and designers are fully immersed in branding decisions, and the marketers, researchers, and customer experts are fully immersed in technology, engineering, and operational decisions.

Keeping in mind that every step and activity are collaborative between all the teams and individuals in this way, the process proceeds as follows:

1. The process begins with the generation of customer insights, using the insight-generation tools and templates described in Chapter 3.

2. Using the customer insights, the cross-functional team agrees on the prioritization of benefits. They identify which emotional and functional benefits are most important to the target group of customers and which ones the team should focus on delivering. This critical alignment step ensures that the innovation process builds the products and solutions that customers will value.

3. With this alignment in place, the marketing team leads a shared definition of the brand domain and the brand value proposition. The brand domain is the market space defined by the highest-level customer benefit identified in Step 2. For example, suppose Apple identifies self-expression as an emotional benefit for its target audience. This benefit can be monetized over a domain that encompasses desktop and laptop PC hardware, personal music players, and software for digital content management ranging from music to still and video photography. The value proposition is the promise that the brand can deliver the high-level benefit of the domain while reassuring the customer through brand credibility and trust to purchase the brand's solution.

4. As soon as the team agrees on the domain and the value proposition, the leadership shifts to the engineers, designers, and technologists to "map" the benefits to the features they can build into the product and service solution. Note that this reverses the typical sequence, in which marketers strive to identify the benefits of products that have already been built. In the marketing-led innovation process, the benefits are identified first and then the innovation supply chain is called on to identify the features that can deliver the benefit.

5. At this step, many innovation projects should be in the pipeline among several brands, products, solutions, and initiatives across the corporation. It is prudent to identify a portfolio of risks and invest appropriately. There should be a mix of big, medium, and small

bets. Big bets are breakthroughs that require high levels of investment and can massively improve the customer benefit and can be highly profitable in sales and margins. Small and medium bets upgrade the product experience and represent less of a breakthrough and a lower investment level. There may be some "shared bets" across business units and brands where investment can be amortized across a broad front. An example is enhanced security for a software company's portfolio of products. All customers will benefit from the increased confidence, and all products' value propositions can be enhanced by the security promise. Each company should balance its portfolio of innovation risk relative to its growth ambitions and include big bets, shared bets, and medium-to-small bets.

6. The long-term equity plan (LEAP) is the planning tool that links the long-term development of the brand value proposition. With an increased pace in innovation, more customers will be even more convinced that the brand can deliver on its promises. The duration of LEAP should be three to five years so that long-term and short-term goals are balanced on a rhythm that's appropriate for the domain—faster-paced for high-growth emerging spaces and slower-paced for established businesses.

7. Next is the tool for initiating specific individual innovation projects in line with the long-term plan. The LEAP may envisage several major and minor initiatives over a three-to-five-year planning period, and each one has an Innovation Brief. This is the document that ensures that the working innovation teams in design, engineering, and procurement (including both internal and external resources) direct their activities to the right target audience. Doing so fulfills that audience's emotional and functional needs based on the benefit-to-feature mapping guidelines and presents solutions that are aligned with the brand's promise.

8. The team implements a discovery process (creative ideation of what's possible within the Innovation Brief guidelines), a design process (turning the creative ideas into conceptual designs of products, services, solutions, and the customer experience), and a delivery process (turning the design into operational reality at the right level of performance and cost). All of these steps include a lot of detailed substeps, collaborative tools, and customer testing. We'll illustrate these in the following Kimberly-Clark case study.

9. The marketing swim lane takes the lead in creating the implementation plan to deliver the innovation plan to the marketplace. The new solution is presented to customers. They are helped with adoption through distribution and channel marketing, and end-user demand is created.

Cheryl Perkins

To illustrate how such an integrated marketing-innovation process can work in practice, we talked with Cheryl Perkins, President of Innovation Edge and former Chief Innovation Officer at Kimberly-Clark, one of the leading executives in the field. Cheryl spent the first part of her career in innovation leadership at Kimberly-Clark Corporation, ascending to the position of Chief Innovation Officer. She was responsible for the company's innovation and enterprise growth organizations, including research and development, engineering, new business, and global strategic alliances. She led a team of innovators to identify and transform insights, designs, emerging technologies, and capabilities into new-to-the-world innovations. Cheryl was recognized as one of the Top 25 Champions of Innovation by *Business Week* magazine (June 2006). She was named a top executive driving vision within the consumer-goods industry (Visionaries 2006) by *Consumer Goods Technology* magazine. She sits on the Board of the Product Development Management Association (PDMA) and the Georgia Institute of Technology External Advisory Board for Textile and Fiber Engineering.

Cheryl is an exemplar of the new breed of marketer-technologists, who represent the leading edge of the new marketing. She understands how to amalgamate science and analytics with customer insight to deliver innovations that win in the marketplace.

"People always ask me," she said by way of setting the tone of our discussion, "is it really possible to systematize the 'fuzzy front end of innovation'? I believe we can—by defining what an insight is, putting a value on it, and making the insight actionable through the insights-into-innovation process."

Cross-Functional Collaboration from the Outset

As a foundation stone for innovation leadership, Cheryl insists on cross-functional collaboration. "It is a principle," she asserts, "that all innovation must be driven by insights, and that insights generation is a multi-lens process. We are trying to understand the demand network of customers, consumers, choosers, and users, and we can only do so by filtering the data through multiple lenses."

And, because insights generation is at the beginning of the innovation process, the "multiple-lens" approach includes the early and consistent involvement of all the individuals and teams who contribute to end-to-end innovation success. Cheryl involves not only marketers and researchers, but also designers, technologists, and financial experts at the earliest stages. This ensures that all of them have a 360-degree view of the innovation process, not just a specialist's view.

Process and Metrics Are the Key

Also from the very beginning, the innovation process is determinedly scientific and governed by rigorous metrics. An insight has value only when it can be turned into a revenue- and profit-generating business action. Therefore, Cheryl Perkins and her team set out to build an insights-into-innovation financial valuation model that could serve as an accurate guide to the value of insights in the pipeline.

"The merit of an insight typically comes from some kind of research score, but we were able to develop a much more complete value analysis. The model identifies what kind of value lies in an innovative solution that is created from a specific insight. We are leveraging all the data mining and past history of what works or does not work in the marketplace to compute the metric. The combination of two scores—the 'research' score of the insight and the measure of the economic value of the solution that comes from the insight—provides a powerful model of cause and effect in the insights-to-innovation process."

Here are some of the key drivers to include in the model:

- Product performance data (such as absorbency performance for a tissue product)
- Sensory data (such as perceived softness for the tissue product)
- Past history of purchase intent scores versus actual purchase relative to this sensory and performance data

- The relative investment cost versus ROI for certain types of functional benefit bundles (such as comparisons of ROI for investing in a packaging convenience innovation versus a product comfort benefit)
- The increase in value available when a higher-level (emotional) benefit is associated with the functional benefit
- Analysis of concept elements and products that didn't succeed in the past (including the value that would have resulted from "killing" these projects earlier)

This is not a casual undertaking. It requires a very sophisticated statistical team to build the model internally. The data and analyses are made available in a web-based application so that everyone on the innovation team has access as a front-page item on their desktop.

Cheryl believes that her model is a practical application that can quickly become a very powerful resource allocation and value measurement tool.

"When we back-test the model against historical performance, we are able to achieve a 95 to 98% accuracy in correlating the drivers of success in innovation with the actual outcomes. I am confident that we can get to that critical point where we can talk about insights and insights-to-innovation in the context of objective metrics that enable us to review the value of each insight not just in isolation but also across a whole portfolio of insights in combination."

In the insights-into-innovation process, insights are converted into ideas. First you leverage both unique knowledge and unique capabilities. Then you convert those ideas into solutions or services that satisfy the customer/shopper/chooser/user needs while also delivering value for the company and its shareholders. The challenge is to design process into the "fuzzy front end" of innovation—to add some discipline but not lose flexibility or nimbleness. It's a balance of disciplined process and creativity.

Discovery: Detaching Yourself from History

The insights-into-innovation process involves three stages: creativity, design, and commercialization. Cheryl calls them Discover, Design, and

Deliver, and she has introduced revolutionary thinking (which she refers to as "detaching ourselves from history") to each of them.

"Discovery requires us to think and act differently so that we can generate new ideas without judging them. We have to design new models to enable us to turn insights into solution ideas that focus not just on needs that customers/users/choosers might tell us, but more on the undermet or unmet needs that they don't tell us about. That's one way to detach ourselves from history.

"Let me give you a creativity example: Caterpillars flex when they move. How does the way caterpillars flex help us better understand how garments should flex? The subjects may seem unrelated, but they may have the same materials characteristics, the same functions, and the same benefits. It's an example of a way in which we get people to think outside the world of disposable garments. We give teams a challenge that's (apparently) totally unrelated to the ultimate innovation task. They analyze the challenge task from the lenses of behavior, habits and practices, functional and emotional benefits, and other aspects. Then we ask them to re-express all of their analyses in relation to a current business opportunity focus. It's amazing how many solutions and ideas result from this process. If you follow a similar process, you'll have no shortage of ideas."

The Centrality of Design

After the Discover step comes the Design step. In fact, Cheryl's approach is to involve designers in the discovery process from the beginning so that they are immersed. Historically, design was often the last step in innovation, limited to putting the graphics on the package before it went out to customers. Design now begins in the fuzzy front end. And, as we noted earlier with the Innovation Brief, a key tool to bridge from consumer and customer insights to the technical intricacies of design is the Design Brief.

"The design process is absolutely essential to making that emotional connection with the consumer. I believe it is a competitive necessity. Otherwise, we'd revert to delivering merely functional benefits.

"Both internal and external designers participate in the discovery and ideation process. At the conclusion of the ideation process, a Design Brief is created. The Design Brief starts with the target audience and the insights on which we are basing the innovation, and the full brand positioning so that all design is integrated with consumer insights and brand strategy. Then the Design Brief provides the specific directions about what it takes to implement a robust idea to meet our target consumers' emotional and functional needs. The brief synergizes function and form and encourages designers to look at all parts of the solution to stimulate all the senses—the visual, the smell, the touch, and the feel. The Design Brief covers the essences of each of the senses to bring the solution to reality for that brand. We work with outside designers who propose multiple options that are evaluated based on the brief and its success criteria so that we start to build a database of the elements of successful design. We build rapid prototypes for further evaluation against the Design Brief and the needs that are highlighted as key drivers in the model."

Delivery Is Just the Final Stage of the End-to-End Innovation Process

After the Design step generates an agreed-upon design that is successfully tested in prototype or concept form with customers/consumers, the process transitions to the development step. In this step, companies look for feasibility and substantiation that the solution can deliver on the brand value proposition, so as to deliver commercialization of a profitable product. Some designs pass through testing and make it through development, with a select few making it into the Delivery phase. It's a process of constantly narrowing the funnel so that by the time you get through the Design phase, you are focused like a laser on development and delivery of that commercial solution.

On the Innovation Revolution

Cheryl Perkins is presiding over an innovation revolution. What we might describe as the "Silicon Valley" view of innovation from the end of the 20th century was technology-, feature-, and performance-centric. That model no longer wins.

"Innovation is no longer about combining math, science, and technology to deliver functionally excellent products. It is now about leveraging creativity and the design process to rapidly create ideas and designs that will deliver a new customer/shopper/chooser/user experience. The key difference lies in making not just functional connections, but emotional connections with those consumers and customers. To win in the marketplace today, the emotional linkage is more critical than the old functional linkage. The consumer experience that we have designed into the new solution must be worth more to the consumer than just the price of technology alone. That's how we achieve consumer loyalty—and premium pricing and margins."

That is why design is so important in the innovation process. Without design it's impossible to deliver the high-level emotional experience to the consumer or customer that is the key to success. When design is applied correctly, it provides signals that really make the solution relevant to the consumer. The signal could come from the user interface, the color and surface design, the shape of the package for a consumer product, a condition indicator, a speed sensor for an online transaction, noise, or taste. The design palette is so broad and subtle that it provides much more flexibility than just technology and pure product performance.

Similarly, the role of research is in the process of revolution. To understand users' experiences and needs, it's necessary to get involved in the usage experience. There is still a place for conventional survey-based market research, but leading innovators like Cheryl are rapidly supplementing and replacing conventional research with design research. They're getting involved with consumers as they use and experience products and services and are turning the observed experience into ideas and new solutions. The technical term for this kind of research is ethnography—the science of observing consumers' and customers' everyday behavior and imputing their motivations and needs from the patterns exhibited in their behavior. Using the Internet, management can automate a lot of ethnographic research. They can observe customers' behavior in terms of the websites they visit, the content that stimulates them to "click through" to the next information screen, their online purchasing and expenditure habits at Amazon.com and Netflix, and the communities they join and online content they read. All of these and other online "behaviors" yield patterns that a new breed of researchers and analysts can project to shed light on underlying needs and the likelihood of future purchases.

The Innovation Revolution Requires Revolutionaries

These concepts—innovation as a process, leading with design, detaching yourself from history—are revolutionary in many companies and contexts. One of the major implications of this thinking is that you will need new people with new approaches, new attitudes, and, most importantly, new skills to lead the way. Cheryl favors the Star Model, shown in Figure 4.2, to guide the organizational design to bring the new innovation approach to life. The Star Model™ is a trademark and copyright of Jay R. Galbraith, the foremost expert in the field of organizational design. Dr. Galbraith stresses that, to successfully implement a strategy, organizational structure and processes must be completely aligned with the people skills to operate them and the rewards for success.

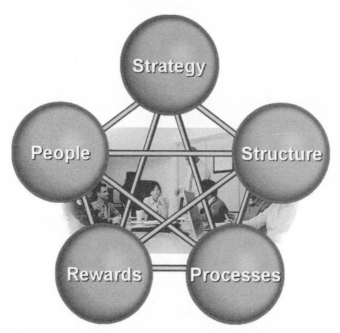

Figure 4.2   The Star Model of organizational design.
©*Jay Galbraith*

As Cheryl explains it:

"One of the biggest challenges is to get the right people who can think in the new way and not prejudge ideas as they are generated. We have found that people with a lot of historical experience tend to prejudge ideas based on their experience. Since innovation depends on generating unbridled ideas and then systematically evaluating them, prejudging is a barrier to the emergence of good innovative ideas. Innovation must be detached from history.

"The skills we have aimed at developing are designed for a new competency. Purely trained 'classical' marketers have a highly developed sensitivity to consumer and customer emotional needs, but it's not combined with technical and design skills. Traditional technologists and engineers are experts in technology and design but haven't been taught to develop their emotional IQ. Somehow, the engineering culture closed off this sensitivity in technologists. I have found that there's a huge innovation productivity win waiting to be seized when you can take a great technologist and unleash their creative and emotional capabilities. Through process, training, and tools, deployed in the right physical environment and supported by the appropriate rewards, it's possible to build a powerful team of marketer-technologists, or customer-sensitive technologists.

"I can't overstate the importance of the people-development role of the innovation leader."

Open Innovation Explodes Your Resources and Accelerates Your Time to Market

How can a long-established company based on traditional approaches excel at the new forms of creativity, design, and delivery? One answer is open innovation and its related innovation systems (see Figure 4.3). Internal processes and internal capabilities may be excellent, but the sooner you bring in an outside view—whether it's from a channel customer, potential partners, or the voice of the chooser/shopper/user—the closer you will be to meaningful innovation. Good ideas can come from anywhere, and it's imperative to get them into your innovation process quickly to get to the most robust solutions and create a winning customer experience. Open innovation really leverages your capabilities via the expertise of others to deliver innovation and growth. Open innovation expands and explodes your internal capabilities and competencies.

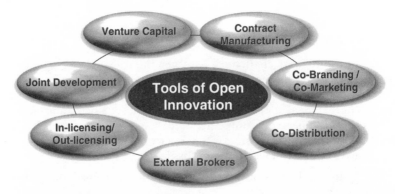

Figure 4.3 The tools of open innovation.
Provided with permission by Cheryl Perkins

Cheryl Perkins describes how open innovation has worked for Kimberly-Clark.

"First, we saw a huge increase in speed to market and also in the robustness of our solution. My favorite example is a partnership between Kimberly-Clark and Sun Health Systems to bring to market 'sun spots.' These are designs on the surface of our Little Swimmers swim pants product; they're shaped like little animals, and they actually change colors with sun exposure. So, if the design changes color, then Mom knows it's time to take her child out of the sun. So not only does K-C have an absorbent product that actually delivers a hygienic benefit, it has now moved into the sun care domain in a way that really helps moms, and provides the opportunity to innovate and expand in new directions. The business team leveraged Sun Health Systems' capabilities and manufacturing, quickly introducing the product to market within six months (versus a couple of years in our historical product development cycle).

"Another open innovation benefit is investments in startup companies. At K-C, we observed them, looked at their strategic and business plans, and then determined if we wanted to invest or actually acquire. The healthcare business is a great example of this. Its focus includes medical supplies and devices, and its benefits include delivering to hospitals the confidence of avoiding the possibility of infection. Microcuff was a start-up acquisition in a ventilator tube with proprietary technology. The business team took it to market because of the advantage it has to prevent ventilator-acquired pneumonia. This was totally consistent with the brand vision and was sourced from outside as a result of open innovation.

"In 2006, K-C created over 50 external partnerships. These external partners have helped minimize internal investment and assisted with regulatory requirements, technical capabilities, and competitive intelligence.

"Contract manufacturing is another example. There's no need to put 'assets in the ground' to bring innovation to market. Clean Team (bath-time products for infants) was brought to market in a very short time by leveraging outside formulators and contract manufacturers. That was a big business model change. Historically, K-C had done everything internally without considering manufacturing externally.

"There is amazing energy in these open innovation success stories. Teams really start to rally around them, because they see the value, and they see that they can bring products to market faster than they ever did before."

The Role of Brand Equity in the Innovation Process

Cheryl Perkins is a marketer-technologist who came up through the technology and R&D sides of the business. But she understands that the role of brand equity is critical in providing direction and context for the innovation process. She suggests that brand equity frameworks guide the innovation process toward the market spaces where the company can win. The brand vision and the overall brand equity framework provide the strategic direction to help the innovation team understand which insights have priority to act upon to achieve the targeted growth level. The innovation process starts with the brand essence and the overall brand positioning, a clear definition of the target audience (including relevant segmentation of that audience) and a deep understanding of the emotional and functional benefits sought by that target audience. The need states are translated into brand domain opportunities. In turn, these are prioritized so that the business focuses on the biggest opportunities to be seized via innovation.

"There are many powerful opportunities for shared bets—growth opportunities that exist across brands. A good example of branding and the power of cross solutions is what the business team did with Huggies. They combined wipes and diapers with the company's Clean Team infant toiletries. Cross-merchandising in a bundle can be powerful. We saw a significant increase in our wipes volume by bundling them with our toiletries products. So cross-merchandising and bundle solutions that deliver the essence of the brand are a critical factor in planning future innovation."

Much of the innovation is in process linkage—linking insights generation to the brand equity development process, and linking both of those processes to the innovation and go-to-market processes. Linking the brand equity development process and the insights-into-innovation processes as seamlessly as possible—including both internal and external collaboration—will deliver the growth that shareholders are looking for.

Risk Management for Innovation

The final ingredient in the successful management of innovation is building a capability to manage risk. Skillful management of risk is a competitive advantage that can be created by being objective and analytical about the risk portfolio. On the one hand, high-risk projects in the innovation pipeline have the potential to generate great rewards via a differentiated customer solution that you bring to market faster and better than any competitor. On the other hand, if your risk portfolio is imbalanced between high-, medium-, and low-risk projects, it's easy to miss a short-term goal because an innovation project got delayed or didn't achieve its targeted adoption levels.

Cheryl Perkins' solution is to face up to risk—to illuminate it and manage it.

"You cannot hide the risk in innovation. You must be extremely open and transparent about the risks and the implications of making a decision. The key is to conduct risk profiling and to train facilitators who can help project the risk. What is the risk to customers, consumers, production, and business profit at the bottom line? It's important to be visible and disciplined and to ask cross-functional teams to examine and assess the risk from the outset so that designers, engineers, and marketers can understand how the financial function thinks about risk, for example. In the past, each individual function would look at risk independently. Now all functions work together to look at the implications of various risks across the business.

"Making risk more visible makes risk more manageable. There is also more discipline. Risks are interdependent, and if you look at them in silos, you will never view the risks interdependently. A narrow view exacerbates the risk and makes it harder to manage."

Summary

Innovation is a hit-or-miss affair for many companies—but it doesn't have to be. In the new marketing environment, innovation can be made more reliable and predictable and can generate a more certain return on the investment you put into it. Here are the keys:

- Genuine customer or consumer insights that illuminate motivations and needs to be met
- Combining systematic process with creativity in order to "design to delight"
- Developing people skills to combine the methodical technological development process with the softer, customer-sensitive creative process
- Placing a financial value on the insights so that you have a portfolio of big bets, shared bets, and small bets to bring to market, and embracing the risk inherent in the portfolio
- Building a collaborative process that involves all the collaborative skills that contribute to innovation from the outset through to the end
- Single-threaded management of the process hand-offs from discovery to design to delivery

A successful experience with innovation is available to every company if you follow these principles.

5

Measuring Consumer Engagement

● What are the causes and effects of the changed communications paradigm that marketers face?
● What are the best industry standards to measure of the effectiveness and efficiency of customer engagement in this new world?
● How can you calculate effectiveness and efficiency in this new environment?

The "last mile" of driving growth through marketing is the customer engagement process. In the new marketing order, all the rules of the road for this last mile are changing.

Chapter 1, "Open Your Mind to the New Marketing," placed the "old marketing" view at the top of the old, aging S-curve (see Figure 1.1), where, no matter how much more effort we put in, the returns in improved effectiveness and efficiency are minimal. Communications is one of the major areas for change. The old marketing communications paradigm was a funnel in which communications such as advertising were poured in, and the aim was to establish user loyalty at the bottom (see Figure 5.1).

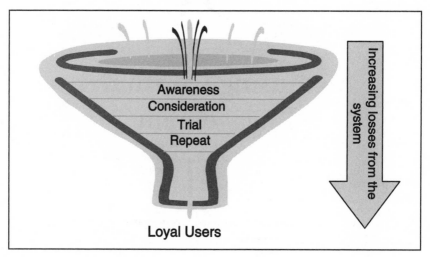

Figure 5.1 Built-in inefficiency.

Clearly, this is inefficient. The system puts in the maximum amount of input (awareness) to turn it—by increasingly smaller percentages—into consideration, trial, repeat purchases, and loyalty. That's the opposite of an efficient process, which aims to maximize results from a given number of resources.

On the new S-curve (see Figure 1.2 in Chapter 1), the old concept of marketing communications (often called "marcom") is replaced by the new concept of customer engagement. Marcom is a one-way outbound concept. We reach customers with short communications, and we hope our messages have impact and persuasion. Engagement is a narrative and a dialogue. We intend to contact the customers when they are willing to listen to our story. We look for response signals indicating that they are inviting us to say more and to enter into the to-and-fro of getting to know them and their needs. Businesses engage customers not only with communications, but with new ways for their customers to interact with them, new types of customer experience, new ways for customers to review and receive the innovations that businesses bring to the market, and new solutions that redefine the relationship.

This new concept of engagement requires marketers to make significant changes in how they approach communications:

✍ **The addressable consumer or customer:** Increasingly, businesses can reach their customers—whether they are consumers of Internet services, shoppers for consumer packaged goods, or manufacturing purchasing agents. A customer can be reached individually at an electronic address as he or she moves between a desktop computer attached to the Internet, a laptop on the go, a web-enabled mobile handheld communications device, or an iPod. Consumers might be using e-mail, Instant Messenger, blogging, knowledge management tools, collaborative business software, or shopping. We can reach them at most times and follow them on the web to analyze behavior that reveals their needs.

- **Customer control over the content they choose to receive:** Advertising—or, indeed, anything that we might typically think of as "marketing communications," that simply interrupts customers before they say "Please tell me something"—is anathema. Engagement is customer-controlled. To engage customers, we must understand their needs and preferences as individuals—or at least in very, very finely segmented groups—and communicate with them when they choose, rather than when the brand owner chooses. Engagement requires personal, individual meaning, and therefore it requires personal, individual understanding.

- **The increased speed of the marketing cycle:** The speed of innovation from new technology development techniques is accelerating to the point that traditional marketing cycles impose unacceptable burdens of delay. These cycles have been based on conducting and manually analyzing research surveys, preparing detailed strategies, entering into long creative-development lead times, and then testing the messages via more research. The innovation cycle makes new products and services ready to launch before the marketing development cycle is complete. Therefore, we need a new marketing development cycle that is equally agile.

The disruptive innovation stage of the new S-curve has three elements. But no standards exist for a new marketing approach to the customer who requires individual addressability, control over received content, and fast-moving, dynamic change. And, you will recall, standards are the requirement before the S-curve can shift from disruptive to stable. If industry standards don't emerge, marketing will never ascend the new S-curve and will remain in a state of uncertainty. How can marketing avoid this condition?

To qualify as an industry standard, a new measurement must have these characteristics:

- **It is defined by the customer:** In the new environment, customers select and control the information they choose to receive and the sources from which they choose to receive it. The marketer can't prescribe the communications channels, such as radio, television, or print, and assume that the medium will suit the target customer.
- **It measures a type of engagement that includes the customer in the equation:** Choosing, responding, reacting—doing something other than just "being an eyeball."
- **It includes all the ways a customer can become engaged from conventional media, to word of mouth and "buzz," to in-use experiences, to encounters with real or digital sales interfaces:** The array of choices is changing and expanding and morphing every day, and the new measurement must be able to embrace them all.
- **It provides a global measurement tool that is applicable everywhere and capable of comparisons across geographies:** In today's global marketing environment, the marketer must be able to weigh the cost and value of a marketing investment in China against one in Czechoslovakia, and a single global measurement standard is required.
- **It accommodates rapid dynamic change:** The customer's list of engagement contacts is continually changing, whether he or she is adding customer-generated content on YouTube, or product placement in a video game, or advertising on a mobile phone. The measurement has to keep up with the customer's changing behavior. Fortunately, with new behavioral targeting techniques and new ethnographical research techniques, we can put the customers in charge of defining the marketing contacts that are most relevant to them.

A New Industry Standard of Measuring Effectiveness and Efficiency of Customer Engagement

Consistent with the shift from the subjectivity of creative communications to the objectivity of standards, leading-edge companies are beginning to adopt a new measurement standard for customer

engagement. One of the leaders in this new field is Oscar Jamhouri, CEO
of Integration Group. Oscar was an ad agency director who worked on
high-profile accounts. He observed the following early in the 1990s:

- The ad industry was failing to address the dynamic changes in the
  communications field brought about by technology and business
  processes.
- Conventional marketing communications metrics, such as
  measurements of consumer brand or advertising awareness and
  "persuasiveness," failed to represent the business model of how
  companies engage customers.
- Mass media communications were actually playing a smaller role in
  engaging customers. Engagement occurs over a long cycle of
  multiple contacts that Oscar's measurement system refers to as the
  Brand Experience. The Market Contact Audit™ (MCA™)
  measurement system by Integration Group has systematized the
  measurement of how effectively a company engages and retains
  customers. The Brand Experience system includes some fundamental
  measures that are surprisingly simple yet profound in their
  application. They constitute what is called a "single global
  currency" for measuring customer engagement, the end goal of
  demand-side management. All measures are MCA consumer
  research-based:
  - **Brand experience points:** Report which marketing contacts
    are important and useful to consumers. In the paradigm where
    the customer is boss, it is critical to know which contacts are
    the ones the customer defines as relevant: a sales call,
    registration on a website, word of mouth, a TV ad, a trade
    show, a sponsorship event, outdoor advertising, radio, or a
    podcast. Therefore, the Brand Experience Points are measured
    in the Six Sigma-based MCA process (Six Sigma is an
    internationally recognized method for quality control
    processes). In the audit, the customer defines the relative
    value of each contact for her needs. The MCA treats each
    contact as if it were a salesperson and asks the following: Did
    the customer get useful information? Did she like or enjoy
    the experience to the point that it changed her attitudes and
    feelings about the brand or category? Was the attitude change

sufficient to change her purchasing behavior? By creating an algorithmic weighting of these cognitive, emotive, and behavioral factors, the system develops a value—a score—for every contact. A total set of contacts, measured by the audit, multiplied by the contact engagement value for each one, results in a total number of experience points.

- **Share of brand experience:** Because this is a "one-number" measurement system, any brand or business can measure both the total number of points it generated with the customer and the share it achieves of all "experience points" recognized by a customer.

- **Experience conversion rate:** The test of marketing effectiveness is not just how well it generates experience points, or even what share of experience points it generates, but how well it converts experience points into sales revenues. MCA data indicates that the average correlation of share of Brand Experience Points to revenue share of market is 0.8. This is a very high correlation score, indicating that a large share of experience points is a driver of marketplace effectiveness.

This conversion rate analysis provides a highly objective view of marketing effectiveness. In conventional marketing, a marketing communications executive might claim for a particular advertising campaign that the rating point total and share of voice were high but that the effect on market share was constrained because of poor distribution by a channel partner or low display levels in a retail store. In the new system, the marketing executive would take a wider view that channel engagement points or in-store engagement points have a higher value than advertising engagement points. The executive therefore might allocate the budget and the creative effort between the two more appropriately.

Drilling down a little further into the analytics of engagement, businesses can develop simple measures of marketing effectiveness. The total number of points by a marketing vehicle (such as a trade show booth or sponsorship of a golf tournament) is an analysis of that vehicle's effectiveness. Businesses can quickly decide which one is more effective and make the appropriate resource allocation decisions.

The total number of points by campaign is a measure of that campaign's effectiveness. Remember, the score is a result of the contacts multiplied by the cognitive, emotive, and behavioral value, so it's genuinely a measure of effectiveness. It's an output measure, not an input measure.

Business managers can calculate their share of engagement points to put their marketing effectiveness into relative context versus competition globally in every and any market.

They can also correlate their conversion of experience points to revenue or to share of market. This helps them measure whether they are more effective or less effective over time and versus competition in the key act of using engagement to close the sale, drive loyal behavior, and raise lifetime customer value. Figure 5.2 shows four widely divergent product categories. Across these categories, the MCA data shows that the correlation between Brand Experience Share (BES) and market share is 0.80 or greater. In other words, for a 1% change in the BES delivered by a brand, there is at least a 0.80 percentage change in the market share of that brand. Therefore, BES is important.

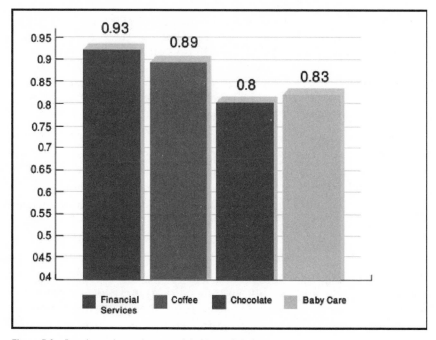

Figure 5.2   Brand experience share correlated to market share.
© *2001 by Integration Marketing & Communications Limited*

Finally, business managers can also measure the efficiency of their marketing effort by calculating the cost per customer experience point in relative competitive terms by measuring their cost per point of engagement share.

We talked with Oscar about the measurement revolution he is leading.

"There are two new breakthroughs in this design of the measure of customer engagement. First, it's a 'single currency' for every contact that a customer has with a brand, whether that is a communications-based contact such as reading an article or a review or a blog, or whether it is an experience-based contact such as a sales call or a shopping mall or a dealer visit, or a usage-based contact such as test-driving the car you're thinking of buying or deploying a new telephone system in a division before committing to it for the entire enterprise. It's a single currency that works and can be compared across all countries. The cost, effectiveness, and value of one 'brand experience point' can be validly cross-compared between Beijing, Birmingham, and Bangalore, and used to make resource allocation decisions fluidly across these markets.

"Second, it's a sensitive-to-manage-with, repeatable, reproducible, empirically proven model with a fundamental track record. It is built on Six Sigma methodologies. In constructing this innovation, we knew we would be assessed on the same principles as finance and production. The system is anchored in the context of the client's business model, underpinned by rigorous activity-based costing and robust data, and validated by case studies."

Procter & Gamble in Europe provides a relevant example demonstrating the business value of this approach. A P&G Beauty Care brand facing low awareness and trial was also struggling with how to apply limited marketing funds to solving its business problem. In-store sampling, mall sampling, and TV advertising were the most utilized marketing tools in the category but were relatively expensive to deploy. The MCA revealed that professional and medical recommendations were among the least-used marketing tools but had a high "clout factor." In other words, they were valued highly by target customers for cognitive and emotive values impacting customer behavior. Using a strategy of focusing on high-clout, differentiating (least-used), and brand-relevant marketing vehicles, the brand shifted funds into driving medical recommendations. In the face of a 20% budget cut for marketing, the brand achieved a +21% increase in share year over year. When it expanded the successful program into an adjacent country, without a budget cut but with a maintained level of spending, the year-over-year increase was more than 72%. *Now that is breakthrough growth!*

"We've audited 7,000+ brands in 183 categories and 60 markets. We know how the retooled approaches to media and communications can impact brand and business results. The system works when clients are willing to take the objective route and apply the science to their marketing expenditures, as P&G did in the example. It fails when there is a failure of decision-making, a reversion to 'guruism.'

"New skills are required to communicate with customers outside traditional boundaries. A key dynamic is that customers have changed the contacts that they consume, not the way that they consume them. They now have contacts from new sources such as the web, from new kinds of word of mouth and expert sources and peer group sharing, from new experiences such as customized interfaces provided by e-commerce platforms. These contacts are new and did not exist in the past. They are additional contacts— the range of contacts is greater than ever. But most marketing measures are limited to testing advertising or the effectiveness of a website or the value of a sponsorship. It is much more useful for a business to (a) consider *all* contacts holistically, (b) integrate them in context so that where and when a contact is made is given the same consideration as the content of the contact, and (c) evaluate them with a single global currency that allows for actionable decision making.

"The results that we have been able to achieve have been in three areas:

- Better focus. In the new fractionated world of contacts, it is easy to forget that 80% of brand experience comes from 20% of the contacts; you win by excelling in the ones that matter and eliminating the ones that don't.

- Greater value allocated to 'intrinsic contacts'—those that consumers or customers cannot bypass, like packaging or design of the branch experience at a retail bank or the 'point of contact' elements of buying a car from a dealership. These intrinsic contacts must be managed and not taken for granted.

- Elimination of waste. The P&G example of focusing on five contacts and eliminating three of them cut 20% of the budget and grew business +25%, eliminated waste, and plowed released funds into what worked.

"From an organizational perspective, the MCA usage has the effect to 'bust silos.' The advertising silo is going to defend the advertising budget, and the sponsorship silo is going to defend the sponsorship silo and not be objective about the relative values. The new 'single-currency' approach promotes 'non-silo' thinking. In a sense, it applies the Asian business culture—a welcoming attitude for shared, collegial, multiple-expertise teams arriving at consensus through objective methodologies and analysis."

Summary

Now customer engagement has a global measurement standard, a competitive assessment tool, an effectiveness metric, and an efficiency metric. Now customer engagement can ascend to the rapid-growth section of the S-curve and save itself from being permanently trapped in the disruptive phase. We are seeing that smart marketers are starting to use the standard, develop stronger analytics, create more robust modeling, and build new variations on the basic theme.

PART **II**

Dispatches from the Leading Edge of the New Marketing

6

Integration of Technology and Marketing

✐ How do you make IT the enabler for marketing to achieve top-line growth?

✐ Why are end-to-end processes superior to point solutions?

✐ How do you get a 360-degree view of your customer through the convergence of marketing and technology for holistic customer relationship management?

✐ How is IT integral to building brand equity to increase customer lifetime value?

Technology is transforming marketing. Historically, marketing has been a technology backwater compared with the supply side of the enterprise. Now it is emerging as the place where IT investment can generate big returns by powering brand-building techniques to drive top-line growth in new ways.

However, implementing this vision is a huge challenge. How does a function that has grown up with creative, ad hoc techniques learn to utilize technology to leverage new models and new processes? How does the organization adapt via new job functions and new forms of collaboration between marketing and IT to enable this transformation?

This chapter explores these ideas with executives from both marketing and technology who have successfully implemented this change to help transform their organizations. From their in-depth perspectives, we can scale the opportunity and define the challenge that faces marketing professionals in harnessing the power of technology.

Let's revisit some of the basic premises of our thesis in this book to frame the case for the integration of marketing and technology:

- Customers—specifically, deep insights into the motivations behind customer behavior—are at the beginning of the brand-led growth process.

- The availability of new types of data, vastly greater volumes of data, and new ways of processing the data can generate new insights.

- The volume and complexity of the data require a new combination of process and technology to accelerate the insights-generation process and to make it repeatable and highly productive.

- The job of marketing is to use these insights to create innovations and initiatives to change attitudes that cause changes in customer behavior that are monetized in purchase, loyalty, and share of requirements. Technology is the enabler.

From Backwater to Mainstream:
Why IT Hasn't Served Marketing Well to Date

We asked Jeff Wysocki, a leader in the field of marketing technology, to explain why technology has not fueled a demand-side productivity surge to equal the achievements on the supply side, and why the situation will change in the future.

Jeff has been a pioneer of enterprise marketing in the consumer packaged-goods industry. At Kimberly-Clark, he was a member of a cross-functional marketing and IT team that designed and implemented new enterprise software called Brand Builder. This software supported marketing productivity in four areas:

- **Knowledge management and sharing:** All marketing and sales practitioners, researchers, product scientists, and anyone passionate about understanding the customer could access the latest information and insights about consumers, customers, shoppers, and users of Kimberly-Clark brands. The information was kept up to date, and new insights and findings were pushed to subscribers to keep them informed and inspired.

- **Work flow and process management:** Processes such as long- and short-term brand planning, annual marketing plan development, new-product launches, and communications campaigns and promotions were all types of plans that Jeff's team envisioned would be managed via Brand Builder. Marketers, ad agency personnel, and salespeople involved in planning could access the software to align the target audience, strategies, tactics, and budgets. Upon approval of the plan, managers could activate the appropriate work flows.

- **Measurement:** No plan or tactic would be "closed" without an attached measurement, tightly related to its objectives and goals. This created success models—complete packages of marketing objectives, goals, strategies, and measures with the associated outcome results.

- **Budgeting and integrated finance:** Both estimates and actual expenditures for marketing activities could be linked directly to the appropriate codes and line items in the enterprise budget management software so that marketing budgets were no longer separated from operating budgets.

Having been a part of launching this prototype of more advanced enterprise marketing management systems at Kimberly-Clark, Jeff moved on to Coors Brewing Company, where he is applying technology to the integration of marketing and sales as IT Business Partner. The U.S. brewing industry is a promising development lab for this innovation because it must integrate demand generation from a large-scale enterprise center. It plans and budgets major initiatives like sponsoring the Super Bowl and buying millions of dollars of TV advertising, through activity to the individual distributors, delivery routes, and bars where the most competitive marketing of beer takes place.

Jeff tells us why marketing has not been well-serviced by technology to date.

"Over the years, I've observed these characteristics of marketing that are barriers to adoption of significant technology:

- Inherently, the marketing organization has more complicated areas, and to build systems to traverse the various areas is difficult.

- Marketing personnel turnover is faster than other parts of the organization. So, you have trouble finding anyone in the marketing organization that wants to take on and own a large-scale technology implementation project because of the duration and the amount of effort required. Unless a Marketing Program/Project Office is in place, your typical brand marketing function does not have the corporate longevity to take this on. There are usually one or two key people within the marketing organization that you can work with to build point solutions; however, usually there are no champions who will want to implement a system across all areas.

✒ Marketing managers may have 200+ data sources of information they use to make ongoing business decisions. Tracking and integrating all these sources of information to make the marketing function easier may be more than IT departments would want to take on.

✒ Marketing leadership has typically never seen IT as strategic. They see finance, sales, and operations groups as partners, but the IT group has traditionally not delivered for marketing.

✒ Marketing does not have common processes in place and tends to be very ad hoc in comparison with supply chain management, who follow standard processes. Auditing ad hoc activities is very difficult."

The result is that marketing has adopted what Jeff calls "point solutions" and never moved toward an "end-to-end solution." A point solution is a request for a recurring report, such as reporting around sales and shipments or supermarket checkout data. At a higher level, but still point solutions, are campaign planning and budgeting, analytics and dashboard tools, knowledge management systems and digital asset management (DAM), marketing mix analytics, and portals. These are all individual tools. One or two of them might be used to manage a specific project, but they do not integrate to create a complete end-to-end solution for the marketing function.

Travel websites are an example of an integrated end-to-end solution. Users can obtain information, set up notifications to receive special-offer alerts, make reservations, buy tickets, and keep a personal profile of their travel preferences. These sites should both increase marketers' technology aptitude as users and support their inclination to build similarly integrated enterprise marketing management (EMM) solutions.

Jeff sees the end-to-end solution as building on these components:

- **Knowledge management, data management, and advanced analytics to improve the insights function:** The system should be able to track and build consumer, shopper, and wholesaler insights and feed downstream processes such as planning with the insights.

- **More integration of the sales and marketing functions via integrated and synergistic solutions:** An example is an integrated sales and marketing calendar. To see what marketing programs each of six company brands are offering to ten different customers across twelve months of activity, a marketing manager may have to consult six or ten different systems or sources of information. By the time the data is gathered, it's out of date. People give up and don't even expend the effort. But as soon as such an integrated system is built, synergistic opportunities emerge that just weren't thought of before.

- **Use advanced analytics and modeling for integrated forecasting, planning, budgeting, and ROI tools:** This enables marketing and sales to assemble credible fact-based plans, budgets, and scenarios and prove value via metrics and ROI. Sales promotion and marketing prove their value and stop being the first budget item to cut when the quarter is below forecast.

- **Integrate CRM (customer relationship management) and DAM, and roll them into an EMM system:** This is the heart of marketing—the external face to customers and the communications assets (logos, package designs, program art, advertising, product sheets, and catalogs). Today, CRM software is not contributing as much as it should to growth because it is not integrated with insights, analytics, best practices, and measurement tools. It's a transactional software that must become knowledge management and process management software. DAM can contribute by ensuring that the right face of the brand and company is presented to customers. An example is enabling a retail customer who is composing a circular advertisement to access the DAM database and select graphics that are guaranteed up-to-date, rather than reusing dated ones from an old storage file on the customer's own computer.

A good example of the potential for an end-to-end system can be found in an activity that is very important to growth in both consumer-products companies and high-tech companies: the launch of a new product. In an end-to-end marketing and sales system, the following are true:

- The insights about the need for the new benefit that's delivered by the new product are developed in the software via the integration of research and analytics. Every downstream participant in the product launch has access to and full understanding of the insight and the benefit. Sales and marketing communications materials are much more consistent and much better informed.

- Product development and product testing results are stored in the system and are linked to the insights.

- Design developments, such as physical form and packaging graphics, reside on the system, fully linked to all other product launch information.

- Product launch success models reside in the system to inform tactical planning so that the right messages run in the right media at the right time. For example, if the success model indicates that four weeks of television advertising are optimal to build awareness of the new product before issuing a coupon for consumer trial, system governance can ensure that the integrated event calendar is guided by such a "rule." If the distribution window in retail stores is narrow (such as for a seasonal product), timing and dependency alerts throughout the system can help ensure that all preparation is timed to meet the window appropriately.

What does it take to transition from point solutions in marketing technology to the end-to-end system approach? Jeff believes that the issues are not technological; they are organizational. He cites the following key factors.

Leadership

"You must have your number one marketer on board. That person needs to understand and champion IT and the program vision. They also need to be a huge supporter of standardizing and simplifying the marketing processes."

Process First, Technology Second

"Map marketing processes and implement the process improvements first, and then deploy the organization structure/changes needed to support the processes, along with the technology solution. Increased ROI comes about with well-executed processes to leverage synergies between sales and marketing. Sales groups can better leverage some of the marketing activities compared with just going off and executing independently. The ability to conduct pre- and post-analysis on your activities is critical, and building in processes to ensure these analyses are done and acted upon helped improve ROI."

Marketers Are Creative People; IT People Are Not

"You need a 'sexy-looking' solution. Your standard SAP entry screen usually does not cut it for marketing people."

Standardization Is a Benefit and a Necessity

"A Kimberly-Clark marketer, when he was transferred between brands, remarked to me that it felt like he was leaving one company and going to another. The required processes on the new brand were completely different than the brand he came from. Simplification and standardization are critical. A good place for that is the marketing annual planning process. We developed templates and combined tools so the marketing people spent their time on the content rather than on the look and feel of the presentation. With a standard format, senior management received the critical pieces of information in a consistent format, so world-class-caliber brand plans were developed."

Efficiencies Can Come from Surprising Places

"You can increase efficiencies for improved compliance procedures for SOX (the Sarbanes-Oxley Act) and improved forecasting accuracy of sales and marketing events, such as coupon redemptions."

Jeff articulates how the integration of sales and marketing should be accomplished from an IT perspective. Now we turn to the Wachovia marketing and IT team, who have led an actual integration, very much spurred by the business strategy of high-volume M&A (mergers and acquisitions) and the integration of acquired businesses. The Wachovia management team has managed one of the most successful brand-building efforts in consumer financial services in the last decade.

Transforming a Financial Services Brand with a New Marketing and Technology Platform

Technology provides the capacity for better insights and the capability to move more rapidly to implement them. You must have a process to make sense of this expansive data and then integrate it into your marketing plans. Wachovia shows how the confluence of data and marketing can achieve a 360-degree view of the customers' attitudes and behavior and can affect their choices to increase wallet share.

Ten years ago, none of this was possible. Marketers in the consumer financial services industry did not have

- Magnetic strip cards widely dispersed throughout the consumer base to capture people's behavior. The data did not exist because the collection methodology did not exist.
- The hardware and software to interconnect the information in a useful, timely manner.

So, a confluence of four factors facilitates Wachovia's ability to market effectively through a new understanding of consumers:

- Sheer availability of data
- Hardware that can store it
- Software to manipulate it
- Analysts to make sense of it all

The marketer's new focus is on knowledge as a tool that, through technology, can be effectively implemented quickly into all the marketing touch points. Wachovia defines this as a *platform*: the confluence of software, hardware, data, and marketing professionals.

The power of the platform comes from the confluence and cross-pollination of data flowing horizontally between Wachovia departmental functions and divisions. The ability to cross-pollinate helps every department and product group understand not just its own business but, more importantly, "the domain of the consumer":

- How do customers' overall life needs affect their needs and behavior in the financial domain?
- Which customers are more valuable to the brand than others?
- Which customer groups represent the biggest parts of the profit pool?
- What actions on our part will move them up the loyalty ladder to choose Wachovia for more of their requirements?

This platform enables predictive modeling. For example, suppose that credit card purchases reveal that a family is acquiring baby products. Historical data analysis shows that having a baby is a trigger for buying life insurance. With the aging of the child, the data tells us to anticipate the need for college tuition. A person aging beyond 55 can trigger a need for long-term care insurance. This allows Wachovia to anticipate need states and extend the customer lifetime value.

In the old marketing paradigm, attitudes toward the brand and product and service categories were the purview of marketers and market research. The new marketing paradigm has an interaction between attitude and behavior that can be calibrated using technology. By understanding the linkage better, Wachovia marketers can increase consumers' tendency to deepen their loyalty and relationships with Wachovia.

Here is how you make the connection between technology and brand building:

- Understand consumer behavior better using the new data streams gathered by the new technologies.
- Apply the new analytics to the data that powerful software can manage—mostly multivariate analyses and cross-pollination of data streams to reveal "if this, then that" analysis.
- Align the insights from analytics with marketing to work on shaping the consumer attitudes that will result in the desired behavior.
- Track behavior to create better advertising and more relevant consumer contact.

Technology enables the tracking of customer behavior while market research captures their attitudes. Marketing professionals can leverage the resulting customer insight to position the brand and communications.

Technology also creates new options for how the consumer chooses to receive the information, and this changes attitudes and behaviors toward the brand. In doing so, technology both creates a new problem and solves it at the same time. It creates the problem of fragmenting the old marketing model; marketing is no longer as simple as it used to be because of this hard-to-manage fragmentation. But technology pays you back by providing more data about the consumer. It also gives you the new channels and capabilities to reach the consumer when the consumer gives you permission to use them—the Internet being the primary example.

The harnessing of technology for marketing requires an extraordinary collaboration between marketing and IT functions.

We know of no better partnership in the industry than Jim Garrity and Bob DeAngelis. Garrity is Chief Marketing Officer and DeAngelis is Director of Customer Analysis Research and Targeting for Wachovia. Working together, they have built a cutting-edge platform integrating marketing and technology. It has helped Wachovia become one of the fastest-growing and most successful financial services brands in a highly competitive category.

In a candid dialogue, they explain their real-world experience in leveraging technology in the service of marketing transformation.

Wachovia management realized they could not cost-cut themselves to business growth. Although this interview illustrates some of the unique dynamics in the financial services industry, that same imperative exists in virtually every business today. Every business has tried to increase its profitability by cost-cutting, but there are only so many costs you can cut. Eventually you must grow, and the only way to grow is by building brand equity using knowledge of the consumer. Garrity and DeAngelis have proven this. So although their experience in financial services may be unique, their lessons apply for all industries.

Here are their extended insights into how to make the marketing/IT partnership work to build customer loyalty.

Jim Garrity and Bob DeAngelis

DeAngelis: We began our data warehousing effort in 1997, followed by building our marketing data mart in 1998. Our objective was to have a high degree of integration of data from across the customer experience and across the company's products. We wanted to bring together related information—transaction-related data, interrelated data, consumer-specific data, and photographic data—into a common platform to build a consistent integrated view of our relationship with a consumer across all touch points over time across all company divisions. The data platform becomes the building block of understanding how to build a customer relationship, which is the unit of analysis around which all the work is done. I don't want to say we have a100% integration across every product, every channel, and every segment. But we do have a relatively high degree—I'd say 95%+ on the consumer side of the house and a little less than 90% on the wholesale side.

It's an ongoing challenge. Complexity increases when we have more mergers and acquisitions and extend our product line; we need to keep integrating those local product views and new business views into the data and analytics pool.

Here is an example we are working on right now. Wachovia recently merged with Westcorp. That deal was completed at the end of last year. In some ways it was almost a reverse merger in the auto finance product area. Westcorp had a larger auto finance business than Wachovia Bank did. We need to integrate the Westcorp auto finance platform into the Wachovia platform. And until we do so, we will not understand that part of our client relationship. For example, is there an auto lending retail client at Westcorp that is also a Wachovia retail banking client? If there is, what other services can we introduce into that customer relationship?

Data and systems integration provides us with a consistent view of the customer relationship, a consistent calculation of profitability, and the ability to support our customer-centric obsession and to maintain it going forward. That's the building block, the DNA of everything we do.

Question: How do you deal with the fact that you don't have a complete view of your retail customer because that retail customer may have other banking relationships or other product-based relationships that are opaque to you? Are you doing various kinds of modeling that allow you to understand what that customer is doing outside of the closed view of Wachovia?

Garrity: Absolutely! Here is how we address that:

- We conduct continual market surveys by geography and product area to understand what our relative share of wallet is, and our relative penetration of the target consumer base.

- From our survey research, we understand that we might have 30% share of wallet. We can classify the 70% we don't have into product and service categories, and the attitudinal and other consumer feedback in the survey can give us the feedback we need to understand how much future opportunity there is from a consumer-need standpoint.

- By purchasing third-party data and putting it through our database, we can infer from investments and deposits what the initial opportunity is from a market size standpoint.

That's where the magic of marketing comes in. How do you take that data, and what do you do on the marketing side of the equation with the Wachovia brand to try and attract those users, either current customers who need new products, or consumers who aren't Wachovia customers? How do you use the Wachovia brand to leverage your marketing knowledge to attract those folks?

Frankly, our number-one priority ever since the Wachovia/First Union merger in 2001 was to retain customers. To really focus on customer service, service excellence, and thereby keep our attrition rates at the very minimum. Virtually everything we did, including our marketing programs and marketing communications, were focused on that objective, and we were successful with that strategy. We are now the industry leader in customer satisfaction, and have been for past five years in a row, with a growing lead. We think it's the one area where we can really distinguish ourselves in the banking category, where differentiation is really difficult.

So, we have a current advertising campaign that's very much focused on our leadership in customer satisfaction and the experience our existing clients have (see Figure 6.1). We believe this messaging will resonate with prospects, and they may think, "If they're that good, maybe I should think about doing business with them."

Now on the metrics side, we will measure the effectiveness of that campaign at the back end. It will include effectiveness of the communication strategy, changes in brand awareness, and changes in consideration, ultimately helping us to understand better the model to acquire customers.

Figure 6.1 Wachovia's current advertising campaign.
Provided with permission by Wachovia Corporation

DeAngelis: We have been tracking our brand since the Wachovia First Union merger in 2001. The goal of the new campaign and positioning was, how do we lead with our strength in service, to emphasize the superior customer experience that generates loyalty? From a domain viewpoint, how do we look at the client relationship being an asset of all Wachovia Bank products and services rather than any particular product or individual business unit?

An example might be that a customer has a profitable banking relationship that's managed at our retail branch network. Our data analysis also tells us that the customer may be a prime prospect for our wealth management business. So there are a whole series of marketing treatments, based on the data that we can activate to extend the relationship. We started to target those relationships with great precision because we are prospecting for thirty to forty thousand out of ten million retail customers who might be good candidates for transitioning. Jim and I were part of that very large corporate initiative pioneered by our CEO, Ken Thompson.

Metrics Is a Part of the Whole Picture

DeAngelis: We're really looking at metrics from three approaches:

- We focus our brand equity tracking on wealthier households, compared with our competitors, by market area. And we look not only at current customers but also prospects; the survey instrument gives us the insight to refine our messaging. So we track the effect of the new campaign on relative awareness, consideration, and preference within key current and target customer segments.

- We look at ongoing message testing. We compare our spots with competitors and best-performing spots and can analyze the effectiveness of messages within the campaign.

- We look at all marketing methods we use and evaluate their impact on customer value, customer acquisition, and revenue.

We learned that the distribution drivers (what happens in the bank outlet) are most important, and within that customer experience at retail, what is most important. For example, we look at the absolute number of outlets in different markets (which influences how convenient our service is for our customers), as well as the staffing level in each outlet (which influences the quality of the experience once the customer gets to the branch).

We were quickly able to learn the relative impact of drivers like this, particularly on driving acquisition and driving revenue. We find that certain factors have a much higher impact on new-account acquisitions, compared with the generation of revenue from existing clients and retaining existing clients.

It's a very dynamic process. The model helps us understand the impact of changing different drivers in the same direction (more branches and higher staffing and higher levels of advertising), different directions (fewer branches with higher staffing and reduced levels of advertising), or any combination. It is called a contribution-to-preference model.

Management is always looking for the perfect, optimum solution. But the marketing mix and the resultant consumer engagement is dynamic; it's inclusive of many drivers, and you can't totally stop one driver without it having an impact on others. Our goal is to ensure we have the right level of consistency and constancy in how we are heard in terms of our advertising message and how we deliver in terms of our customer experience.

The model also tells us when we can actually reduce our investment in advertising in a particular market without negatively affecting sales, and when we can invest in another market where there'd be a higher return. Basically, we could achieve a higher level of growth in a short period of time by balancing our geographical mix. We were able to demonstrate that for the market where we reduced spending there was no negative impact on sales, and we were able to reinvest in another market and generate a preliminary indication of upward revenue movement in that market.

The Value of the Brand

Garrity: I think that five to six years ago there was not much appetite for investing in marketing, particularly in advertising. Management just intuitively felt we had to make some investments there, but none of them had any good idea of what an appropriate investment level would be. A unique opportunity for us was to build this Wachovia brand "from scratch," going back to the launch in 2002.

Internally, we created literacy around the value of the brand, and the cost to build one, particularly because of the relative lack of awareness of the Wachovia brand. At that time, financial-services companies were becoming much more brand-oriented and investing in their brands. We felt the competitive heat to create a brand that would be competitive with others. Management now believes that we need to invest in this brand. Marketing, and advertising in particular, is now reinforced by data at this point.

DeAngelis: For the last 25 years, given the degree of consolidation via mergers and acquisitions in our industry, in essence, we all became cost-reduction-driven as opposed to revenue- and customer-focused. That began catching up with us. Deals now are usually larger. At Wachovia we consolidated a hundred mergers in 18 years with a major new acquisition every year for the last few years.

So there emerged a new imperative: The way to win isn't by cutting expenses, but to build a brand for long-term share appreciation, incremental revenue, and year-upon-year growth in the same retail units.

This imperative focused us on the unified view of the total customer relationship—both current product usage and the insights that customer research could bring us about future and unmet customer needs and preferences. M&A consolidation is a business strategy, but our customers don't care about that. They are focused on basic human aspirations such as wanting to be known, and to feel valued.

We found, through our data analysis, that the majority of our customers transact through multiple channels (retail, mail, phone, Internet, etc.). Those who use financial centers tend to be very attractive to us. We believe the in-person experience, even in this age of automation, really has a lot to do with customer satisfaction in building our brand.

When we were high on the cost-reduction strategy, there were programs in place to encourage customers to use alternate channels. Now we realize that bricks and mortar and our employees' smiling faces, with their well-trained approach to serving customers, are a huge brand-building asset for us.

Books of Business

DeAngelis: We use a tool we call the book of business to provide a fully integrated view of the customer relationship across products and channels. The goal is to equip the frontline salesperson, or customer relationship management person, with a holistic view of the client relationship. The idea is that the client expects us to know them whether they just dropped in at the branch, but half an hour ago they were online.

The book of business is a ledger that can track six years of all our contacts with a customer. We can then model from this customer database all the transacting patterns of all those households. And we look at what branch, if any, they are most likely to use for transactions. We also know their primary address, and we take the clients that are most likely to be transacting and are in close proximity to a particular branch, and we assign those client relationships to a team at the branch. We do an annual analysis, and then we assign that book to the branch once a year. On a monthly basis, we share with the branch changes in the customer relationship, as well as a lot of interesting marketing information, and all sorts of marketing leads. We also generate reports of how much the business grows—in terms of total balances, in terms of numbers of new relationships, and in terms of retained relationships. The results are reported versus goal as part of the incentive compensation system. What we've done is leveraged the underlying information and patterns in a way that directly affects the pocket wealth of the branch staff based on how well the customer portfolio performs. So there is a continuous information and compensation loop that supports this retail process.

Now let's look at the employee behaviors. The employees recognize over time, once they understand this system, that it is no problem for them to personally know every member of every family in the book of business. They can go out of their way to ensure that the customer has an extraordinary experience—to know them by name, to recognize them when they walk in the financial center, and so on. It's kind of like the old friendly banker on the corner, but one that's really smart, and enabled through the technology platform.

The technology is set so every teller has the screen in front of her/him. When the customer comes into the branch, there is a fair amount of information that could lead to a discussion that will be perceived as a benefit to the customer, because the bank service person can offer suggestions for additional services or advising services they might want.

The Changed View of Marketing at Wachovia

DeAngelis: Much of this development in the sophistication of our marketing and IT systems stems from a defining moment that transformed the perception of marketing. We were faced with two kinds of customer attrition as a result of the mergers in which we had participated and the customers' perceived issues with branch service. Through IT and data we were able to measure the problem, and through rigorous analytics we enabled the process to understand it. That was the impetus that gave rise to the corporate centers of excellence in customer analysis and marketing. It would mitigate future losses through the frontline staff at the branch and through customer contact. We were able to develop metrics and refine solutions, and we've been able to measure the incremental fiscal benefit in the billions of dollars on a regular basis. Senior management supported the investment, and they became aware of the critical nature of the brand in the success of the Wachovia/First Union merger and the building and maintaining of the brand equity in the post-merger period.

Garrity: During the formative month, when we were putting together the Wachovia/First Union merger plan, we knew how many millions of dollars were required to build the new brand, pretty much from scratch.

This was considerably more than either company had ever spent. We were totally accountable for this large amount of money, and I think that was an early catalyst for the partnership across three functions: the customer analytics group, the finance group, and the marketing function. At the same time we presented the case for the investment, we also presented a case for centralizing governance, a case for how we would be accountable, and demonstrated the return on the investment over time. I think that was the beginning of marketing credibility, which we've built and strengthened ever since.

The CEO Commitment

Garrity: Bob and I have had a great experience under the leadership of Ken Thompson, the CEO, who's been in charge through this whole process. He had a vision that inspired us to become the leader in customer satisfaction. We all perform according to that vision, so every employee understands the importance of taking great care of our customers.

Ken's vision also foresaw the potential benefits of a First Union-Wachovia combination. He had been chairman at First Union. Ken clearly gets the credit for the leadership that has driven Wachovia to be so successful over the past five years. His vision was for Wachovia to be the most admired and trusted financial institution in the country. And I think by many metrics we have been able to achieve through his leadership.

7

Open Innovation and New Product Development Through Communities of Practice

- How can communities of practice help spur open innovation?
- How do communities of practice create an agile organizational culture?
- Why is generative change more sustainable than mechanistic change for organizational development?

New technologies have combined with new organizational paradigms to accelerate the speed and focus of innovation as a solution to customer needs. A new field of "open innovation" brings together communities of practice (COPs) to solve specific innovation problems, as discussed in Chapter 4, "Translating Insights into Innovation for Brand Financial Growth." Marketing has become part of the COPs movement in developing open innovation through two principles:

- The new marketing is not a departmental function or a specialty within the enterprise. It is a core competency driven by collaboration and knowledge sharing across multiple functions and departments.
- Creativity does not depend on special people enjoying aha moments of inspiration. Creativity is the output of a process that frames objectives in terms of meeting customer needs and then arrays all available resources against achieving those objectives.

COPs are a simple but powerful strategy for knowledge-based innovation. Link a number of people with a like interest, skills, experience, and knowledge. Give them some time, attention, resources, and the appropriate motivation. Then turn them loose to collectively solve a business problem through open discussion and sharing. The technology of the web has enabled COPs to become a critical organizational change tool to create growth.

COPs are changing how multinational corporations relate to the consumer, as well as how the internal/external organizational culture is evolving. An organization can now rapidly acquire and apply new knowledge to introduce new solutions to customers. The new imperative is the creation of knowledge capital. COPs accelerate the pace of learning and generating new capabilities.

This chapter presents a special perspective on COPs from Procter & Gamble.

Larry Huston, retired, former P&G Vice President for Innovation and now Managing Director of 4inno, talked with us about the new "Connect and Develop" innovation process that leverages the resources of scientists and innovators both inside and outside the walls of P&G. He explains how P&G has totally restructured its innovation efforts around this organizing concept to improve speed to market and scope of innovation. Connect and Develop is a terrific example of how COPs can be used to engineer the product development process.

Larry Huston

Larry Huston knows about marketing. In conceptualizing new businesses, he knows that the critical element is to understand the directions in which consumer needs are migrating. He facilitated the P&G CEO Innovation Leadership team for six years. He also headed Innovation for P&G's worldwide fabric and healthcare business before he was given the task of figuring out how to create a significant discontinuity in P&G's innovation capability. While Larry was in this position, the Connect and Develop program was conceived and implemented. The Connect and Develop innovation model is based on a clear understanding of consumer needs. P&G has created a process, engineered through technology, to link a set of identified needs to promising solution ideas throughout the world. P&G applies its own R&D, manufacturing, marketing, and purchasing scale to create better solutions, faster.

CEO A.G. Lafley established a P&G goal to acquire 50% of P&G innovations outside the company. The strategy was not meant to replace the capabilities of the 9,000 researchers and support staff, but to better leverage them. The program has been a great success:

- In 2006 more than 45% of P&G's new products in the market had elements that originated outside P&G, up from less than 10% in 2000.
- More than 50% of the initiatives in the product development portfolio have key elements that were discovered externally, allowing P&G to meet its goal of 50%.
- R&D productivity has increased by 60%.
- Innovation success rates have doubled, and the cost of innovation has decreased.
- R&D as a percentage of sales is down from 4.8% in 2000 to 3.4% in 2005.
- P&G has now launched more than 250 new products from which some aspect of execution came from outside the company.

The program began to show results slowly and over time has accelerated to increase top-line sales by billions of dollars.

Specifically, when Larry commenced the program, four new products were introduced in the first year to April 2002. From April 2002 through June 2006, P&G introduced more than 250 new products.

Clearly this strategy has contributed to P&G's sustained and steady top-line growth. Between 2000 and 2006, P&G's share price increased more than 150%.

We asked Larry to speak with us about the dynamics of the Connect and Develop program at P&G.

The Goal Is Brand Building

Larry stresses that, in the Connect and Develop process and community of practice, P&G is driven by the same strategic goals as the totality of its business. These are the goals of brand building—what will meet consumer needs in the framework of a brand capability or brand image, and what will differentiate the brand in the eyes of the consumer. Everything starts with the consumer. Consumer understanding—when it is superior to that of competitors'—will drive brand growth. The understanding of consumers is expressed in the form of insights about the consumer needs the brands aim to meet. Then the Connect and Develop process swings into action:

- The process translates insights into a tool called a *technology brief*.
- The community of practice is tapped to identify individuals and companies globally who have skills to contribute to answering the brief.
- Internet communications and social networks as well as physical contacts are utilized to reach the qualified individuals and companies to try to obtain the answers.

The Internet becomes the great enabler. It facilitates finding the best resources globally, because with the right kind of searching tools and technologies, Larry's community can find people who have answers that match the problems the briefs are aiming to solve. Larry calls it "creating a fingerprint" of a specific product problem in a technology brief. The system has access to public information on each scientist's patents and published articles and can match scientists with technology briefs. Data processing technologies and sophisticated search engines are turned loose to make a match between the desired technology and the people who might have possible solutions.

As Larry puts it:

"The Internet and search engines enable us to find 'a needle in a haystack.' Finding the right people to address a specific product brief is a needle-in-a-haystack problem. Ten years ago you could not even find the people; you did not even know who they were. Consider that in our business areas, we now have 1.8 million people who are eligible to work with us. Ten years ago, we did not even think externally beyond our 7,500 P&G R&D specialists."

The result is an explosion of available resources for any company in any business.

"The Internet has reframed our mind-sets about what is possible. Each industry can contract legitimate companies that can estimate for them how many outside scientists and resources there are for their area of enterprise. For example, the auto industry has about 3 million outside resource people who they could conceivably tap for product and service innovation."

The Aha Experience: Humility in the Face of Global Talent

Resources are not all that's expanded. Larry finds that the thinking and mind-set of the company that enters into COPs behavior are also expanded.

"We learned how good and smart the outside world is—much better than we initially thought. Executives at large companies tend to believe that they have a lock on the best talent because of their big recruiting efforts. We are successful at attracting some top talent, yet you can be blinded into believing you have captured all the top talent. The reality is there is tremendous talent all over the world.

"The P&G advantages that enable us to compete and win in the marketplace include our business model, our scale, and a variety of factors including talent. Some folks have a tendency to zero in on the idea that the reason you are winning is primarily because of people. While people are important, there are many other systematic processes in place that drive competitive advantage. So I think we have learned a lot about the quality of the talent outside and become a lot more humble."

The Cost-Benefit Equation: Creating Value

As with all the innovations in business process and business models that we have highlighted, the community of practice can be harnessed to output measures that ensure that you get a return on the investment you make in this tool. In this case, there is a network effect. The network includes not only the company and its partners in the community of practice, but also the channel customer and end-user consumer, who all must benefit for value to be created. The network also includes the shareholder, who must see the return on investment in the form of earnings growth. Larry is acutely attuned to value creation across the network.

"At P&G, we try to maximize the value-creation potential of our external relationships via risk-reward agreements. Fundamentally, we are measuring the value of what we receive in the exchange versus what we are paying for it. We want to be fair for the outside partner and fair for P&G and our consumers. If we have a discovery project underway, does it have the ability to generate sufficient value for the consumer, P&G, and the partner? The name of the game is to get into as many relationships that you can handle where value can be created. So we measure partnerships by value creation, and we measure productivity at the network level: what value are we getting out of our hub in the U.S. compared to hubs in Europe, India, Japan, and Australia? Is the productivity up to par, or are we missing opportunities?

"One of the productivity metrics we use is the percentage of solution ideas that come from different regions of the world based on the resources they have. We look at the intellectual property assets in these regions of the world and how we are leveraging them to solve consumer problems. For example, the U.S. network contributes three times as many ideas as the European network. However, the European asset network is larger than the U.S. Specifically, the world's chemical industry is located in Europe; there are 38,000 chemical companies in Europe. If we are getting as many chemistry leads and ideas out of the U.S. as we are from Europe, then we are missing an opportunity to leverage a lot more out of Europe."

Building Networks and Leveraging Assets

Managing a community of practice is like being a farmer looking at plots of land and determining how to get more productivity. P&G is leveraging the world as an innovation landscape, and really harvesting ideas from all parts of the world. It avoids the tendency to overwork one region to benefit from the diversity of working all the regions of the world. This fulfills the promise of a truly global company.

From his global perspective on the community of practice that he oversees, Larry Huston takes a different view than Thomas Friedman, author of *The World Is Flat*:

"The world is spiked, not flat. For example, I received an e-mail from someone in the Chilean Ministry of Economic Development, and they are trying to figure out how to move Chile out of being a commodity economy: copper and agriculture. Chile has less than ten patents. Procter & Gamble has 30,000 active patents. One little part of P&G has more patents than the whole country of Chile! The world is heading in different directions in terms of utilization of intellectual capital. Look at China and India or even Italy and Germany, where the name of the game is identifying the relevant intellectual property assets and measuring your country's ability to leverage those IP assets to create growth. It is not so much measuring people as measuring the total network."

A New Role: The Technology Entrepreneurs

In a fully aligned company, the organization is highly tuned to the execution of strategy. In this case, the strategy in question is to leverage the community of practice to achieve growth via innovation. To leverage the power of the network, P&G created a new organizational role: technology entrepreneurs.

"We have 70 of these technology entrepreneurs, each of whom reports into a business unit in the global regions. We have virtual networks and physical networks, where people who are located in regional hubs make contacts.

"It's important to have a physical as well as virtual contact. If we tried to access ideas from India through the Internet, it would not be nearly as powerful as having our technology entrepreneurs in Mumbai and Bangalore. Our technology entrepreneurs have their own community of practice; they participate in our own discovery community with a flow of information. They produce a catalog that we distribute to our organization of hot ideas they have found from around the world. They are the ones in charge of putting technology briefs together. They also develop the metrics to measure the number and quality of products that they brought in from the outside. So they have highly robust roles; they are more than scouts. They are strategic thinkers, ambassadors, scouts, and have many other roles. Many have ownership of nodes outside of P&G. Some might own a lab or an invention shop. They operate within their business unit and operate as a team in the technology entrepreneur community of practice. We move things around at lightning speed. It is a very lively interactive community."

Internet-Based Companies That Facilitate Innovation Are Part of the P&G Constellation

Companies such as Nine Sigma, InnoCentive, YourEncore, and Yet2 all utilize the Internet in innovative ways to help match talent to problems. There are probably three hundred similar companies; invention and talent markets are an area of rapid development. Not many multinational companies have really adopted this concept of invention and talent markets yet. P&G has been a market-maker in this arena. Larry suggests that this provides a great opportunity for new users of these markets and networks to achieve breakthrough growth.

"We are still in the early stage; all of the Internet-based technology exchange companies have available capacity because there are not many takers."

Marketing Is Behind

Larry views what he has been able to achieve via the community of practice approach in a very objective and tough-minded way.

"In the end it is not about the tools. What are the results? We all have such tremendous pressures and mandates. You have to have a tough, results-oriented mind-set. You can't become enamored with ideas, but you have to become enamored with the business results."

He also has a challenge to the marketing community.

"What I've described is the Community of Practice for the matching of consumer needs to technology solutions. It's a critical part of marketing, but it's not the entirety of marketing. The commercialization and go-to-market stages are the other parts of marketing. For innovation to work effectively, every link in the chain must be equally strong. I have thought hard about how to apply the principles of Connect and Develop to the rest of the marketing function, but the thinking has not yet fully permeated the whole P&G organizational development.

"Communities of Practice, value-creation networks, and internal/external linkage represent the future. Marketing, as a function, is significantly behind. I would love to see more interest in this area by marketing people. There is a tremendous amount to learn. Look at a business such as the U.S. cigarette industry that continues to build its business without any direct advertising—no TV and print and billboards. Brands in the industry have grown their business because they have found new ways to communicate to and motivate the consumer. They are continuing to build communities. Marketers in the auto industry or consumer packaged goods should be saying, 'What can we learn from the marketing practices in the cigarette industry?' There are so many industries to learn from.

"Marketing people do not approach their jobs in as structured a way as product developers, because they have not been trained in the scientific method. It is not part of their professional rigor, as it is for scientists. Marketers do not focus on what will be the next big discontinuity; how do I create a network? I think the 'Connect and Develop' idea probably will have more impact over time in the marketing area than it has had even in the product development area; there are just so many more assets to leverage in marketing.

"I do not think there is as much curiosity and not as much practice of the scientific method among marketing people. Where are their communities of practice? Who is building the marketing networks? Do they even know what the issues and principles are? I daresay many companies don't.

"For the Connect and Develop initiative in innovation, P&G made a strategic commitment. It is rare that a company would assign a VP, give them a large budget, and say, 'Go and figure this out.'"

The world is waiting for someone to do so in marketing.

Bill Veltrop

Having talked with Larry Huston, we asked Bill Veltrop to put Larry's ideas about COPs into the larger context of organizational change to drive growth. Bill is a leading "evolutionary agent" in the fields of organization design, learning, and change. He contrasts "generative change" with the more traditional mechanistic approaches. He touched on the ways in which COPs support generative change.

The generative-change approach treats organizations as living systems. This is in contrast with a mechanistic approach, which is more of a "recipe orientation."

The key in generative change is to think not just about what organizational capacity you want to put in place, but about what is needed for this to be manageable as a system.

Bill suggests we need to ask these questions:

- What kinds of practices and processes need to be put in place?
- How do you align the reward system to support new practices?
- How should these processes steadily improve to become self-sustaining?

"If you develop and support existing and create new communities of practice to enhance, accelerate, and facilitate organizational learning, it can be one of the most inherently generative change strategies that you could utilize.

"COP should be a part of every change initiative, because it adapts to the reality principle that the most effective learning is social. COPs are very natural and informal—they break out of the training box. So that particular learning strategy supporting individual and organization learning is one of the basic ingredients I would use in any developmental change initiative.

"Generative change represents a crucial shift from the mechanistic worldview that has historically dominated organizational thinking. The evolution of communication, connectivity, and capabilities as a result of the web is rapidly moving us to where we can have the equivalent of not only face-to-face interactions remotely but all manner of tools that support collaborative work. This provides a rapid and tremendous opportunity: to take communities of practice to a radically new level of effectiveness to enhance the sustainability of any kind of organizational change."

Communities of practice have expanded the corporate collective intelligence quotient by enabling inside and outside resources to collaborate to bring innovation to the market faster and cheaper. To make this work, organizations must achieve generative change so that the new practices can take hold and be sustained.

8

Brand Building Through Global Brand Growth

*/ How do you capture both explicit knowledge and tacit knowledge in one place and make them useful for global marketers?

*/ How can a global brand keep a single personality intact while presenting consumers with different expressions around the world?

*/ How can you maintain brand authenticity and still change?

*/ How can global metrics be used to manage brand growth?

Even businesses in mature, flat categories can achieve breakthrough growth by reigniting their brand value and top-line growth by global expansion of distribution.

A brand with universal emotional appeal can be a powerful platform for international growth. The brand equity investment really pays off in rapidly growing markets such as India, China, and Eastern Europe. Many associate brand equity with specific business categories such as consumer goods or fashion; however, brand value is a universal driver of growth and profits in every category. Engineering marketing to increase brand value is based on maximizing the relationship with desirable consumers to increase engagement, loyalty, revenue, and margin. This engineered relationship is the key to profitable growth whether your brand is IBM, GE, Chevrolet, Tide, Qantas, Mittal, Kit-Kat, or a server farm solution from Sun Microsystems. The relationship can be understood through the principles of consumer engagement, consumer loyalty, and long-sustaining revenue and margin cash streams:

- **Consumer engagement:** Chapter 5, "Measuring Consumer Engagement," explained that consumer engagement is one of the best measures of marketing success. We can define engagement by measuring relevance, cognitive, affective, and behavioral variables. The brand engages the consumer effectively when it offers a relevant benefit or solution, supported by the right information that is easy to access and consume, and when the offering results in a positive shift in or reinforcement of brand attitudes and perceptions. This shift in attitudes leads to positive consumer behavior to purchase. Consumer engagement is secured when the right target audience is identified; the message is communicated distinctively, authentically, relevantly, and accurately; and the delivery of both information and brand experience achieves "right time/right place" status.

  We can measure this (via consumer engagement points) and apply analytics of share, effectiveness, and efficiency and translate it into revenue and other outcomes.

- **Consumer loyalty:** Consumer engagement is the sum of the attitudes and perceptions the consumer holds about the experience he or she has had with the brand, whether through use; via communications; or in an information exchange with a referral, a salesperson, or a website. These attitudes and perceptions are monetized when they translate into consumer loyalty—purchasing more consistently, with greater frequency, and with the allocation of a greater share of requirements to your brand than to your competitors. This is the consumer behavior that we seek to achieve as marketers when we focus on improving brand attitudes.

- **Revenue and margin:** Brands that generate strong perceptual attitudes also drive fast, long-lasting, less risky, less volatile cash streams. Similarly, well-perceived brands can raise margins relative to their peers and their categories via both pricing power and the ability to change the unit mix to include more premium-priced components.

This chapter demonstrates how the Jack Daniel's® brand generates global growth in a mature category (whiskey). Jack Daniel's management capitalizes most effectively on global consumer insights, and they harness those insights to generate astonishing growth momentum.

"The Globalization of Jack"

There are debates over whether marketing should be more creative art or more business science, but for Jack Daniel's, balance is a particularly strategic imperative. The Jack Daniel's brand legacy is an artistic interpretation of a history that began in the mid-19th century and extended into global 21st century relevance with an emotive and engaging message. "Under the hood" is a rigorous application of management science, metrics, and groundbreaking technology utilized to establish and sustain Jack Daniel's as a leading global brand.

In the mid-1990s, Owsley Brown II became Chairman of Brown-Forman and ignited his vision of a global Brown-Forman with the Jack Daniel's brand as the launchpad. We don't know what Mr. Brown's wildest dreams were, but he may have succeeded beyond them: from 0 to 200,000 cases sold a year in South Africa, and from 200,000 to almost a million cases sold in the U.K. Jack Daniel's passed the 120,000 case mark in China in 2005. Growth in the United States has also increased. The international sales share of total sales expanded from 10% in 1985 to 46% in 2005. The surge in "the globalization of Jack" is probably the most exciting development for the brand in the past two decades (see Figure 8.1).

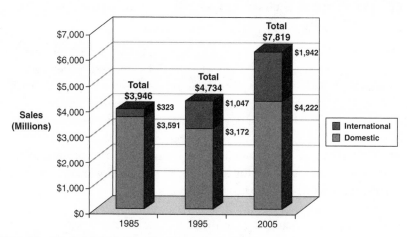

Figure 8.1　How Jack Daniel's® world has changed.
Provided with permission by Brown-Forman Corporation

We asked Mike Keyes, Global Managing Director for Jack Daniel's, to provide his perspective on how brand values and popular culture have contributed to the Jack Daniel's persona and taking Jack Daniel's global. He also discussed how technology has enabled Jack Daniel's to communicate with the consumer.

Mike Keyes

Mike Keyes is one of the world's most experienced and accomplished beverage marketers. He has studied the complex and subtle emotional relationship of consumers with their alcoholic beverage brands of choice. He also has studied the equally complex world of multitier distribution through licensees, wholesalers, retailers, on-premises bars, and off-premises retail stores. He has guided brand building through most forms of local, regional, and national government regulation that the bureaucratic mind can design. Few people can aspire to his level of command in his field, and, because he loves his work as much as he does, to his level of professional satisfaction. Mike is a member of the Brown-Forman team most associated with the "globalization of Jack"—the establishment of a powerhouse brand that has achieved astonishing heights of success at the global level of competition.

Applying Process, Technology, and Metrics to Grow Jack Daniel's Globally

Mike describes the early years of international expansion for Jack Daniel's as "relatively easy" to manage. The market target was the "American abroad" or others, such as tourists returning from United States visits, who had been exposed to the authentic American Jack Daniel's. A small United States brand management team could define the strategy and a set of rules for transferring Jack Daniel's brand communications to foreign countries. They were able to manage the brand's substantial growth for a long time by simply making the Jack Daniel's brand available to those who knew about it.

However, this simple "rule book" approach does not work today. The target market has changed to millions of global users who may never have been to the United States, and whose emotional connection to the Jack Daniel's brand is based on a new set of contacts and contexts. Also, the marketing team has changed. As Brown-Forman opened offices in Hong Kong, Seoul, Cape Town, and Prague, it recruited new teams of marketers who were exposed to the brand heritage for the first time.

They were professional marketers but were not yet steeped in the history or culture of either the Jack Daniel's brand or the "Brown-Forman Way" of global brand building.

Brown-Forman faced the challenge of transferring tacit knowledge—from the top management team who had "lived" the brand for many years and held its traditions, history, and essence—into explicit knowledge. This is the codified, organized, accessible shared knowledge that constitutes the intellectual property on which the brand's future would be built. Mike relates his view of the challenge.

"We have hired over twenty new Jack Daniel's marketers in the past two years in Europe, Eurasia, and Africa. How do we get these people up to speed to feel the passion, intuition, and understanding of Jack as quickly as we need to?"

Process and technology help provide the solution. Brown-Forman created an ordered and disciplined marketing knowledge center with technology to support knowledge management and dissemination while investing in the creation of new intellectual property. This enabled the marketers to use institutional knowledge and consumer insights to build the Jack Daniel's brand systematically wherever it was distributed.

"First, technology and the processes of designing and building a marketing knowledge center enable us to immerse global marketers as quickly as we possibly can in the Jack Daniel's heritage. We categorize consumer attitudes about our brand and share lessons that we learned from our consumers and consumer tracking—what our consumers are talking about and how we communicate with them to create and reinforce their sense of friendship with the Jack Daniel's brand.

"Second, we utilize a process-based Brown-Forman Way of Brand Building, because we no longer can exclusively lead the brand globally with a small group in an intimate, intuitive way. As the brand becomes more global, process becomes more important to managing it. The B-F Way, currently Version 3.0, provides the process for all of our marketers around the world to become our brand champions."

Mike describes an "old world" of brand strategy meetings that were intimate and less process-driven because decisions were made intuitively by a small group of highly experienced people. In the "new world" of marketing planning that integrates global and local planning—with local plans developed in different languages, often with interpreters—

brand strategy development must be much more process-driven. And a matrix organization must be created to operate the process globally.

As Mike explains:

> "The challenge is to not become so process-driven that you lose the creative magic inspired by history, heritage, and intuition about the Jack Daniel's brand. We address this through a core Jack Daniel's global team here in Louisville: a business strategy analyst, creative director, creative manager, consumer insights expert, and me. For the past four years, two of us have played a leadership role in the various strategy and ideation meetings in each of our regions. So you get this nice balance of people who understand their market, and people who understand how the business is structured, and a process that enables them to work together from a shared playbook. The global team members are the gatekeepers for the Jack Daniel's heritage and history, and through knowledge sharing and process-based collaboration, the local market teams also become better gatekeepers for Jack Daniel's. The balance can't be maintained without process."

The Insights-Led Process Should Define the Brand Culture So That a Diversity of Cultures Don't Define Your Brand

> "You learn very quickly in global marketing that your brand people abroad have a natural inclination to emphasize their market uniqueness. As I enter their market and share what has worked for us around the world, the first thing people do is tell me why and how their market is different."

The global brand team responds to this naturally strong tendency by developing tool kits of marketing programs for local marketers to choose from. Whatever they choose will be within the acceptable parameters of the translation of the Jack Daniel's brand.

> "Our biggest challenge is to have our marketers embrace brand attributes that we have in our Jack Daniel's toolbox and for them to choose which are applicable to their market rather than simply trying to create new ones. So we have to achieve a balance of Jack Daniel's history, heritage, and its actual cultural dynamics and even its legal dynamics with the reality that every market reacts differently to beverage alcohol. Sometimes we can be too rigid in how we view the brand without sufficiently understanding the culture, and sometimes our people abroad can be too parochial to

open their eyes to see how Jack Daniel's may in fact have some global brand-building techniques that are wonderfully powerful in their own market."

"The solution to this organizational tension is—as always—to be consumer-centric and gather insights through consumer research and observation. Managing the intellectual property that is the Jack Daniel's global brand in a local market is delicate, but critical. You hire the best and brightest marketers and put them to work in the marketplace, be that China or India. Does their business school education cause them to prefer change over the preservation of heritage? Does it qualify them to interpret the local popular culture in the right way? The best way to avoid the risk of misinterpreting the brand to the local market is to provide the marketers with the consumer-centric insights process. Also important is our insistence that country marketers learn the brand's story; visit its home; and study its roots, origins, and all the cornerstones of brand building."

One Global Brand Personality—with Different Expressions

"There is this wonderful tension between the messages we send and popular culture. One of our lessons learned about Jack Daniel's is that the brand personality registers strong attributes on *authenticity, honesty, and integrity.* This can be translated into *positive rebellion* or *living life on your own terms.* Look how Jack Daniel's is used as a prop by Hollywood and the popular culture in the United States to portray something about character. Jack Daniel's-type characters tend to be masculine, strong, and, whether bad or good, tend to live life on their own terms. But we see the idea of self-independence interpreted differently around the globe. So, a very smart, highly educated Asian brand manager will say, 'You know, Mike, that won't work in Asia. Everything about Asia is a little bit different with regards to independence; people here try their best to fit in and work very hard to not be independent or be perceived as on the fringe.' We actually believed that for a period of time, but our ethnography in the market enabled us to develop the insight that it was not true that people didn't want independence or to live life on their own terms. It's just that the Western measure of expressing independence may be different. So being independent in a small market in Southeast Asia may be very different than being independent in Chicago, Illinois.

"So, in Asia it might be just a different haircut. We may think that is minuscule, but Asians are likely to think it is major. The way this translates to Jack Daniel's is that the consumer may spend a large amount of their income to go to a bar and buy a bottle of Jack Daniel's—it is served in many markets in Asia by the bottle—just so they can set it in front of them in a nightclub. People will look at them and say, 'Wow! That person is very independent, and that person is living life the way they want to live life—they are a trendsetter.' This is something we at first had a hard time getting our arms around. But we know now that we have to understand Jack Daniel's attributes in a cultural setting. We do so by developing insights from observed behavior and research."

Similar lessons have to be learned directly from consumers and applied in other areas of brand imagery. Take graphics as an example. The Jack Daniel's graphics are based on the iconic black-and-white Jack Daniel's label. As a result, most of the brand's messaging and point-of-sale materials around the world tend to be black-and-white. However, in parts of Asia black is a symbol of death. Posting billboards with a black background and white letters is something consumers in those countries aren't used to, consciously or unconsciously, and they find it shocking and upsetting. In those markets, Jack Daniel's altered its out-of-home advertising beyond a simple black-and-white campaign. A global brand should not defy the local culture.

Another similar example of balancing "the brand's world" with the realities of what Mike call's "the drinker's world" concerns the imagery of the original distillery in Lynchburg, Tennessee. One of the icons of the distillery is the famous tour guide, dressed in overalls and a straw hat, representing authentic heritage and rural pace of life.

"In the United States, the imagery creates this interesting attention to a real place that's very different from the urban markets—the last respite from the frenetic pace of life, a beacon of relaxation, where you can catch your breath, and your cell phone won't work.

"The problem, for example, is that in parts of Romania a tour guide's appearance might actually have been too close to what the people are trying to escape from. So while 'down home' is a universally virtuous attribute in developed urban markets around the world, it may not always be a positive attribute for folks who are just emerging from rural economies and rural life. We let the consumer make the decision, and we simply downplay 'down home' in Romania for other pertinent brand attributes."

Despite the exceptions, the bigger insight is that universal attributes, benefits, and messages can be found.

> "Another powerful need that I believe is universal, that our brand tends to satisfy more than most brands, is the need for genuine friendship. Jack Daniel's messaging is about trust and civility and what these values stand for—delivered with an authenticity that we call *tell, don't sell*. We try our hardest not to cross a boundary with our selling messages that would put us "in your face" or "ask for the order." We believe consumers "get it"; they personify Jack Daniel's, and they call for "Jack" by name."

The Importance of Metrics in Managing Global Brand Growth

Jack Daniel's brand teams can manage positioning, marketing, and messaging systematically across the globe using process and technology. The third member of the triumvirate of global growth management is measurement. Metrics become more important than ever as global brand owners like Brown-Forman face up to the challenge of global marketing resource allocation.

> "When brand sales were 85% in the United States, it was easy to understand how we would expend our available human and financial resources to grow the brand. But the brand is now in over 120 countries. We have to be smarter about how we continue to grow the brand and how we grow our other current and future one million case markets around the world."

Mike suggests that four factors measure global brand growth metrics:

✐ Focus on brand consistency and continuity by sending consistent brand-building messages that resonate around the world. This requires investing in the development of a consistent brand-building model for the company's global talent to utilize.

✐ Develop adaptations of the model in countries and regions, and apply them in pilot form as proofs of concept. Demonstrate that the model actually works on the ground and qualifies for investment. China provides a good example.

> "We have developed a brand-building model in China that combines tactical choice, channel selection, and geography focus. We grew the brand on-premises (nightclubs and bars) in large and midsized cities around China using promotion rather than

advertising. We developed the model collaboratively with our Chinese and Asia Pacific in-market teams, activated the model in a controlled fashion, and collected the results. From there, we were able to build the business case to sell the corporation and local team on investing a larger percentage of resources against China."

- Become expert in data collection, data analysis, and data modeling to effectively allocate resources. The global team might develop similar models for Australia, Brazil, or Russia. It must be able to measure accurately the return the brand can generate market-by-market and overall in the short, medium, and long terms from the resources it allocates to the operation of the global brand-building model.

- Underpinning the successful application of these strategic disciplines are highly talented marketers who are motivated brand champions in every country and who are aligned with global brand process disciplines.

"As the brand grew in the early days, we were less systematic in allocating people and dollars in potential markets. Now it is becoming incumbent on us to take an analytical and strategic approach: we have to be right about it, we have to measure it, and we have to adjust. We have to exercise this approach to decide not just which countries to invest in, but also what programs to invest in. Is it above the line (advertising) or below the line (pricing and promotion)? Is it on-premises, is it off-premises, or is it more feet on the street?"

This is precisely the point in the marketing process where data and technology start to make a massive contribution. In a global brand-building environment, there are inevitable variations in the amount and quality of the data that is available. Point-of-sale purchase data streams, panel data, and other standard forms of information flow are just not always available. The analytical and modeling tool kits must be able to adapt to and deal with these different data environments. Global currencies such as the brand engagement point methodology (refer to Chapter 5) must be developed so that a measurement unit in China can be compared directly with a measurement unit in Brazil or the United States. Technology in the form of statistical packages, advanced analytics, and data modeling must be applied to develop priorities from a vast range of brand, country, channel, and program data results.

In data-rich environments such as the United States, the same technology and analytics can help the brand make resource allocation decisions that support groundbreaking innovation.

"We are in the third year of our NASCAR program, the largest single program that Jack Daniel's has ever sponsored. We believe it is important that we put the proper metrics in place to make sure we are getting a rewarding return on our investment. Before we extended an agreement with Richard Childress Racing, we conducted an in-depth consumer tracking survey to determine whether our NASCAR involvement was helping to build our core brand measures. It showed we were getting more NASCAR fans and people in NASCAR markets—not only in the United States but around the world—interested in our brand. So, it has been the most in-depth program measurement undertaking that we have ever tracked. We track not just intent to purchase, but also our image attributes and ratings on key predictive measures such as "Is the brand for people like me?", "What brand I would recommend to a friend?", and, very importantly, "Is it a responsible brand?" We use exactly the same metrics in a tracking study that measures the same variables everywhere around the globe. In this way we can make local investment decisions (like NASCAR) from a global framework and manage a very complex set of choices. We can also measure long-term values such as brand equity so that we never risk the long-term future of the brand by eroding its equity for short-term sales results."

The success of NASCAR/JDTW (Jack Daniel's Tennessee Whiskey) partnering in the U.S. led to a similar new 2006 sponsorship in Australia with V-8 racing.

You Can Maintain Your Global Brand Authenticity and Still Evolve

Jack Daniel's brand essence lies in its history and authenticity. In the "world of the drinker," the brand essence also revolves around its role of making friends in a contemporary, fast-changing global setting. How is it possible to balance these two vectors? The solution is to separate the delivery medium from the brand message and not confuse the two. While the brand essence is unchanging, the selection of media and communications, and how consumers choose to consume media, is changing dramatically. Policies and practices must keep up with the change. Mike cites a simple but dramatic example.

"If you click on NASCAR.com, you will see that the Jack Daniel's brand is very visible and very active on that website. It is an enormously popular website, because NASCAR fans around the globe come here to get their information. Featuring the Jack Daniel's brand on a website other than our own is just something we have never done before. However, making friends with NASCAR fans is important to brand growth, and so we have to be flexible enough to make sure that our policies don't put hurdles in the way we keep up with our consumers. We've not only initiated a presence on the NASCAR website; we've evolved it. Every Friday on NASCAR.com, for example, Clint Bowyer, our driver, writes a letter about what's going on in his life. This is consistent with our guidelines of trying to be friends, or telling versus selling; we give our consumers a look into Clint's life and his challenges rather than just trying to sell Jack Daniel's. This whole idea of just keeping a wonderful dialogue with consumers, in new modalities and contexts, with a voice that is authentic for the Jack Daniel's relationship, is a really interesting everyday challenge for us."

The Harvest of Brand Equity in the Global Marketplace

Mike Keyes points out that not many spirits products are truly global brands; they may be available globally, but they do not communicate the same brand experience everywhere. They may lack investment in a global brand framework or the rigor in its implementation. Mike suggests:

"At some point in time, for many other brands, sadly someone cut a corner or someone positioned the brand in one country in a way that's not even similar to the positioning in another country, or someone discounted the price of a brand that's positioned as super-premium elsewhere in the world."

These practices are destructive to global brand equity.

There is immense long-term cash flow and profit stream from the investment in global brand consistency, supported by processes, frameworks, data, metrics, and technology. After the global platform is built, the brand team can enter new markets such as China—not by reinventing the brand for the market, but by adapting a global toolkit and success model to local consumer and channel needs. As soon as the measurement system is in place, the brand team can make informed decisions about both level of investment and marketing mix.

"We have proven that Jack Daniel's is able to achieve an attractive return on investment in each of our expansion markets because we've invested in brand equity and we are diligent about maintaining it. Technology really has begun to help us succeed. Today, we do more of our research through the Internet, so we can talk with more consumers very quickly. We can show consumers advertising and ask for their reaction. We can test cross-geography and cultures so that we are not communicating in ways that upset our consumers, but confirm they can relate to our messages. This is how we adapt quickly yet don't change our foundational building blocks.

"While Jack Daniel's is rooted in both our production locale and the 'drinker's world,' there are very few new Jack Daniel's marketing managers who, when they first see some of our Lynchburg-based advertising, featuring the whiskey makers, say, 'Boy that's just what we need in my market.' They are so used to ads from other alcohol beverage brands being either more rational or more based on lifestyles or the latest fashions. But we demonstrate scientifically and through business results that Lynchburg advertising can create a wonderful platform and tension with what consumers see and hear from other brands that it actually shows how differentiated—in a positive way—our brand is. When we first enter a market with the traditional Jack Daniel's approach, the local marketing teams are skeptical, but many would kill us if we ever tried to take it away now. That's the power of the global brand framework, technology, process, metrics, and global brand equity."

9

Growth Through Brand Portfolio and Risk Management

* What are the tools and techniques to optimize resource allocation across a portfolio of global brands?
* How can a brand portfolio manager increase return on investment through brand renovation?
* How can the CEO take leadership in asset allocation modeling for brands?
* How can business process and technology transform the perception of the role of the marketing function in the C-Suite?

Every CEO and CMO in a large multibrand corporation has the same challenge. Given a portfolio of brands, countries, initiatives, and marketing investments, how does the brand-owning company manage the maximization of current and future growth across this complexity of opportunities? This is the challenge that Brown-Forman Corporation, the company that owns Jack Daniel's®, manages every day in every country in the world.

Mark McCallum is Brown-Forman's Chief Brands Officer. While Mike Keyes is applying the advanced mathematics of resource allocation models to Jack Daniel's in its global markets, Mark is charged with adding another dimension to the financial Rubik's Cube. He manages a portfolio of 40 brands that vary according to global, regional, and local distribution.

Mark views as a challenge the need to apply the marketing process to every one of those brands—to obtain and refine insights and to apply those insights to develop products, communications, and a brand experience that drives loyalty, revenue growth, and margin growth. He measures the return on investment for each brand in every country, and he allocates resources to maximize the current and future value of the Brown-Forman portfolio. Not easy when every brand manager is yelling, "More for my brand!"

A single brand is an asset that yields returns to the corporation. If successful, the brand provides faster and more profitable cash streams, at a higher level of reliability, and with less volatility than the benchmark measurements of its category. A portfolio of brands is a combination of risks and opportunities. It has as much complexity as a hedge fund or a "fund of funds." For hedge funds, increased risk is balanced against higher returns. For index funds, lower, more controlled risk achieves market levels of return. A portfolio of brands is positioned somewhere between a hedge fund and an index fund. Brown-Forman leadership would like to achieve higher than market returns—fast growth, high margins, better future earnings prospects—to be rewarded by Wall Street through a higher stock price and better shareholder returns, yet with controlled risk. That's exactly what a well-managed and well-balanced portfolio of brands at a company like Brown-Forman or P&G can provide: higher returns than the average in the market, with a controlled and acceptable risk level.

Let's see how Mark McCallum does it.

The Mission of the Brown-Forman Portfolio

Brown-Forman Corporation is a portfolio company with 40 brands of alcoholic beverage products. The company is the sum of the strength of those individual brands within the portfolio. The company's mission as a brand builder is to strengthen company capabilities and performance in building the individual consumer franchises for every one of those 40 brands in the portfolio in every country and market in which they operate. Each individual brand leader understands that she or he is charged with the accountability of strengthening the consumer franchise for that brand. The company measures brand value and return on investment capital (ROIC) as trailing indicators of the strengthening of the brands franchise and rolls them into a portfolio of financial returns.

A portfolio approach allows the company to proactively balance the investment in brands that are growing fast and some brands that are "under renovation." Brown-Forman monitors a dashboard of brand health measures with data gathered through brand tracking. Brand health measures focus on leading indicators such as differentiation and relevance for the target audience. There is a clear relationship between brand relevance to the consumer or target audience in any country and predictable future success.

Super-Premium Margins:
The Key to Portfolio Management

The financial return on a portfolio of brands is highly governed by the pricing and margin mix that is represented in the portfolio. Consumer packaged-goods companies typically operate a portfolio with a range of price points and margins. Look at P&G, whose portfolio runs from laundry detergents like Tide to premium beauty products like Olay Regenerist and SKII. Portfolio mix management also applies to owners of consumer electronics brands and business-to-business technology brands. Every quarter, Wall Street analysts comment on the gross margins achieved by each corporation, reflecting the portfolio's pricing and margin mix. One of the tasks of marketing is to continuously rebalance the portfolio in favor of the premium end of the margin mix by targeting the right customers with the right innovations, experiences, and messages.

In the spirits industry in North America and other affluent markets, successful marketers have produced significant growth in super-premium brands in categories such as vodka, bourbon, and tequila. Jack Daniel's is a great example of a brand that's been able to maintain a premium image in a traditionally nonpremium category (bourbon). It continues to develop its brand equity by increasing its value perception with a select but nevertheless large global target audience.

"Why would a consumer pay $35 for a bottle of Grey Goose or $22 for a bottle of Jack Daniel's? They do it because it is an affordable luxury, and the brand messaging around Jack Daniel's has evolved with this societal need for affordable luxury. There are plenty of other brands in the Brown-Forman portfolio that don't qualify for 'premiumization.' The majority of Canadian Whiskey brands have not been able to ride the wave of 'premiumization' because they either have not been renovated correctly or never had the brand equity to be able to 'premiumize' it at all."

The Portfolio Return on Investment from Brand Renovation

As Mark McCallum thinks about optimizing investment returns, he must make informed and objective choices about which brands can or can't realistically be renovated and elevated.

"It is absolutely possible to renovate brands.

"Not all brands are equally productive, but the renovation components are the same. First, you have to believe that you can move your brand pricing upward. If that's not possible, then renovation is probably not worthwhile, unless it was already a high gross profit brand. Renovation requires investment. We have our metrics on brand value added and return on investment. If you can't predict on a 10- to 20-year projection that you can get positive brand value and get above 9% return or above weighted average cost of capital, then it's probably not worth undergoing the renovation."

In Mark's portfolio, every brand is charged with strengthening its own consumer franchise. Then Mark makes the linkage between the value of the consumer franchise and the brand's investment potential. He uses the analogy of a club.

"The only reason a consumer wants to join your 'brand club' is because you are communicating with them in a voice and with a message relevant to them. If we are to be successful in attracting members to a brand's club, it's because we say something to consumers in our invitation that they thought made joining worthwhile. Then we must continue the dialogue with that consumer in a way that retains them as a member of that club. A brand steward's job is to attract more and more desirable club members as they steward their brand forward."

The relevance of Jack Daniel's to its "club members" is constructed on the idea of male independence. As Mark says:

"There is a huge consumer need today for that confident, independent male—the 'alpha male' feeling. If the brand speaks and behaves as the personification of that feeling, then it is relevant to those who seek to fill that need.

"If your brand relevance is based on an emotional benefit, then your brand can thrive for generations. But if it's a functional benefit (such as trendy or inexpensive), you are only as good as the next innovation."

The Scientific Method of Resource Allocation

A portfolio company like Brown-Forman has a different resource allocation challenge than a mono-branded company like United Airlines or even Nike. Brown-Forman has to divide resources among 40 brands before it even begins to decide how to spend within each brand. A major leap forward for Brown-Forman has been to create the universal model for resource allocation across the portfolio.

"This breakthrough has been unbelievably empowering for us. In the past five years we have developed a resource allocation process and tool that has been extremely powerful in its ability to ensure we are feeding the right mouths."

According to Mark, it's not so much rocket science as "blinding logic." The resource allocation model itself is a software-enabled multifactor analytical tool based on factors such as historic performance, predicted future performance, geopolitical considerations, and critical measures such as the brand's current profitability. Those major quantitative and financial factors are combined with attitudinal brand equity measures in what Mark calls "the final factor." This enables the Brown-Forman management team to combine the mathematical formula output from the model with their management judgment based on considerations such as brand health scores, proven test results, and intuition.

A helpful step in the construction of the model was the creation of resource allocation blocks called "brand-market units"—the combination of one brand and one market. For instance, Jack Daniel's in Germany is an example of a brand market unit, as is Finlandia vodka in Australia. Brown-Forman has developed a modeling of quantitative factors that enable the potential return comparison between the Jack

Daniel's–Germany unit and the Finlandia Vodka–Australia unit and any another brand-market unit.

> "We develop a working estimate of all financial resources available for brand-building activities. We then run multiple combinations of brand-market units across the globe, and the model shows an optimized allocation of resources against those brand-market units."

The quantitative model does not have the last word. The management team, as a group, applies brand-building skills, business judgment, and intuition to the outputs. For example, Brown-Forman might not have brand history in a developing market such as India. As a result, the quantitative model might indicate no action in India. Yet, management understands qualitative factors about India and assigns the market an important initiative value. For example, it's important to the brand-market portfolio strategy to develop expertise in a large, growing, and potentially "premiumizing" market such as India. Therefore, management decides to override the model and develop the Indian market in an appropriate way with a long-term view. The model is adjusted appropriately and rerun.

Case in Point: Jack Daniel's in China

Mark uses China as a good example of long-term considerations overriding the model's output.

> "With China, there are some macro indicators that it will deliver the targeted return on our investment. We put aside the conventional view of the large size of the market. What we focused on was that China decided in the mid-'90s to encourage capitalism within its own country. Suddenly, the global driving concept of 'premium and ultra-premium' was now part of the consumer dynamic in China. Spirits brands became a 'consumer badge.' There was a very significant consumer segment extremely interested in affordable luxury, and our premium spirits are perfectly able to be a part of that quest in China. Jack Daniel's imagery fits a global need-state of independence. This was a combination written in heaven for us."

Thus, Brown-Forman marketers could predict a favorable long-term future based on the analysis and extrapolation of global trends integrated with specific emerging consumer attitudes in China. However, consumer marketing cannot operate in a vacuum. Regulatory and political barriers must be overcome, and distribution channels and logistics must be developed. The Chinese government only recently has allowed even the importation and marketing of foreign premium spirit brands. So, with the combination of gradual regulatory change and a massive consumer attitude and behavior shift, Brown-Forman made the portfolio bet for a strong long-term return on investment in the Chinese market for Jack Daniel's and its other premium spirits brands.

The risk factor in investing in China is higher than it is elsewhere, so Brown-Forman must review the risk-reward ratio. A favorable capital structure is considered in this decision.

"We are favored in that we are not like a brewery or a car manufacturer who has to inject enormous capital in order to start up. We export Jack Daniel's from Lynchburg, Tennessee, and we export Finlandia from Finland. We do not have high capital investment at all in the Chinese market, and so most of the risk discussion has been always around the ability to repatriate revenues and earnings. One of the hedges against that risk is our dramatic growth. Essentially, our premium brands entering a market that is opening up to the idea of affordable luxury, expressed by consumers' spirits choices, have the potential to be profitable very early in their life cycles. We are in value-creation territory from the beginning. As much as we could do scenario planning on the very significant risk factors—regulatory, social, economic, or macro-side risks—we have invested in our brands at a pace that is sensible and doesn't expose us from a medium- or long-term value perspective. Simply, we have never doubted our ability to create brand value in China."

The Role of Leadership: Owsley Brown and Resource Allocation Modeling

As Tom Falk of Kimberly-Clark points out (see Chapter 16, "Empowering Change from the Top Down"), marketing, when it is viewed as the key driver of revenue and profit growth via demand generation, requires CEO-enabling leadership. Mark McCallum describes how Brown-Forman had been blessed with that leadership.

"Brown-Forman Chairman Owsley Brown is a unique and extraordinary business visionary. He was a sort of a prophet of resource allocation. Game theory and the quantification of risk have always been a fascination of his. I suspect Owsley had a resource allocation model in his head twenty years ago and it has taken some time to convince the entire organization, or at least those opinion-formers within the organization, that it is as useful as it has proven to be. He was the principal early influencer within the company of resource allocation through this combination of highly quantitative modeling and management intuition and judgment. It is fair to say that the Brown-Forman leadership team are passionate disciples of this strategic imperative for our business success."

The acceptance of quantitatively modeled resource allocation is a very difficult behavior change to make in any organization that is not used to managing that way. Most companies build units of independent thinking or operational freedom that become increasingly less inclined to want to listen to top-down direction or top-down mandatory decisions. Owsley and his team gently but firmly applied the leadership tools appropriate to overcoming the natural resistance by focusing the discussion not on *whether* to manage via quantitative resource allocation modeling, but *how* to do so most effectively.

As Mark recalls:

"It took us a few years to 'iron the bugs out,' and we made significant reallocation of resources to brand-market units. There were some that had been able, in the prior era, to just continuously increase their budgets; all of a sudden they were faced with very strict resource allocation criteria, and perhaps that brand-market unit didn't qualify for their 'usual' increase. That's problematic from a change management viewpoint—it takes a lot of hand-holding. We traveled those markets, explaining to our global market teams that, 'Yes, that's all their business is worth allocating at the moment, but here are the criteria for attracting more allocations, and you should be testing all sorts of ways to improve your brand performance in order to attract resources.'"

In this way, the application of the model, along with talented and persuasive leadership, generates not only efficiency (the right dollars spent against the right opportunity set) but also effectiveness (competitive efforts to qualify for greater resource allocation by proving the investment benefit and ROI by developing and testing many new brand-building ideas).

Brand Value

Comparing a portfolio of brands held by a brand owner to a portfolio of stocks held by a financial investor is perfectly valid. Ownership of a financial asset provides the holder with a return that derives from that asset's future cash flows and earnings. The price fluctuates, depending on the market perception about the reliability and risk in those future cash flows and whether they will grow or decline with extended longevity. Certain brands in the consumer packaged-goods sector, such as Tide and Clorox, have been generating reliable cash flows for many decades and can be expected to continue doing so. Several of the Brown-Forman portfolio brands enjoy the same status as reliable future cash streams. Mark McCallum's brand managers play the role of stewards of those future cash streams, and therefore are the stewards of brand value. They are building financial assets.

"No brand I have ever worked with has the long-term financial value of Jack Daniel's. There may be others, perhaps, that could claim similar consumer loyalty—such as Nike. But the market needs to see whether the iconic value of Nike can last several generations. Within the spirits industry, we can benchmark the asset value of brands because several have been acquired over the last three to five years, and it's public knowledge what was paid for them. The acquisition value is often expressed as a multiple of the latest twelve months' sales revenue. The multiple that Jack Daniel's would attract would be extraordinary—considerably larger than the multiple many acquirers have paid for reasonably strong brands in the last five years. Not many people would challenge the fact that Jack Daniel's may well be the strongest brand within the entire spirits industry.

"Building strong brand equity in the local market can generate new cash flows in the global market to potentially make the multiple value even higher. Because Jack Daniel's enjoys ever-strengthening consumer equity in many countries, it creates potential relationship equity in new markets. Distributors in those new markets are eager to make Jack Daniel's part of their distribution portfolio.

"Not only will these distributors carry Jack Daniel's, they will also take other Brown-Forman brands in our portfolio that we would expect to develop in that market. There are many examples of our other portfolio brands riding the 'coattails' of Jack Daniel's in developing markets. Therefore, the equity value of Jack Daniel's is not calculated on the future cash flows from JD alone, but also on the relationship value and channel access value it generates across our whole portfolio."

Business Process and Technology Are Key to Brand-Building Success

Mike Keyes describes what process has achieved for Brown-Forman in the globalization of Jack Daniel's and the creation of the equity value that Mark McCallum is managing. Process engineering also powers the whole portfolio of brands. The Brown-Forman Way of Brand Building is a continuously calibrated methodology of how the company builds a brand—any brand, in any country.

"It is essentially a process guide for anybody whose work 'touches' a brand at Brown-Forman, whether that individual works in marketing, sales, finance, production, or anywhere else in the corporation. It covers everything from environmental analysis, to brand architecture, through strategic development, ideation, and marketplace activation of programs. As the Brown-Forman business grows and the number of those who work on our brands around the world grows, it is incredibly important that everyone in the company understand and respect this process.

"We exercise the process in a way we call tight/loose: tight from the point of view that we do have process and we follow it, loose from the point of view that we celebrate brand building as a true blend of art and science. That imagination and creativity are equal partners with process and analysis in the quest for ever-stronger consumer franchises. The Brown-Forman Way is the guiding code for how we go about the development of our brand business plans. Most of my time is spent just trying to gently instill processes, and it is terribly important that I am not interfering with what I call 'creative ideation.' The process is working really well for us."

Technology supports process.

"The whole resource allocation model itself is technology-enabled and mechanical. We couldn't have run this black-box model a few years back, but we can now.

"Another impact of technology is that we are brand building interactively now. Through technology we can invite and delight brand club members or franchise members. Our reliance on mainstream media resource allocation has certainly decreased. Our ability to communicate with our consumers directly and say things relevant to them and then engage them in dialogue is helped immensely by the technology available to us now.

"There are unique challenges in the beverage alcohol industry because of regulations, but every brand in our portfolio has a very active website, and many have very relevant consumer response programs to engage in conversation with consumers."

The Role of the Marketing Function

Is marketing a function that has equal weight with other functions in the corporation's decision-making boardrooms? There is some debate in the broader marketing community about its "seat at the table." Mark McCallum's method at Brown-Forman suggests yes. When brand building is built on a strong process backbone, rigorous financial criteria and the tools to apply them, and the technology to operate both processes and financial metrics efficiently and consistently, marketing influence can compare favorably with any other function or business discipline.

"All I can say is that, at Brown-Forman, it is just inconceivable that the brand stewardship function is not a significant voice at the table. As we together set strategy for the future prosperity of the organization, it is essential that the voice of the brands be articulate and audible."

10

Insights-Led Brand Building in Technology

- How can technology companies build an emotional component into their brands?
- How can technology companies work with the insights process?
- How can global technology businesses harness global insights to build global brands?

Some categories and brands do not have a tradition of building emotional connections with their users. As a result, they have not unleashed the full power of insights to sustain the customer engagement and loyalty that provide long-term, reliable cash streams. Although consumer packaged-goods companies such as Procter & Gamble and Brown-Forman are well versed in how to connect emotionally with consumers, large technology companies are not. A great technology brand such as Microsoft may have good brand recognition but not necessarily the deep emotional loyalty that brands in other categories have developed over years of careful cultivation.

When a technology company tries to build a brand "from scratch," it has an opportunity to overcome the historical absence of emotion-based brand building by introducing an insights-led process from the outset. We will illustrate this point with a case history of Windows Live. Peter Boland, as the former Global Brand Director for Microsoft's Windows Live brand, utilized the customer insights process to build a new brand loyalty among consumers who know Microsoft but who might not yet feel an emotional connection to the brand.

Microsoft was founded in 1975 and was one of the most successful growth companies through the 1990s. Today, financial markets perceive Microsoft as owning mature brands (such as Windows and MSN), many of which operate in slow-growth categories.

There's a saying in marketing that there are no mature brands, just old thinking. As Mark McCallum pointed out, any brand can be reinvigorated—its equity can be monetized in emerging new growth areas. The limiting factor is whether an acceptable return can be made on the investment in doing so.

One of Microsoft's most powerful and well-known brands is Windows. Its successive relaunches as Windows 2000, Windows XP, and, most recently, Windows Vista, are front-page global news events. Windows has a huge share of its category and has enjoyed a long and fruitful relationship with millions of customers. Yet, even a juggernaut brand like Windows must face transitions of a magnitude that require significant marketing-led change.

The latest big change for Windows is the shift to a hybrid online-offline model. Although software loaded onto the hard drive of customers' computers is still a huge business, customers want to access some services online. Sometimes, their need for access is "all-online," such as when they are mobile and need computing services via their cell phone or wireless laptops. Other times, they may need both online and offline capabilities simultaneously. For example, they might want to use the power of the Windows operating system on their hard drive while also accessing an online service such as web e-mail, instant messaging, or search.

The Windows answer is a brand extension called Windows Live. The "Live" suffix is attached to a number of Microsoft offerings, including Xbox Live and Office Live. It connotes a new level of connectivity—online access to Internet services. Windows Live is a platform for consumer online services including web e-mail, Instant Messenger, search, and safety tools. Microsoft knows from extensive research that, for many consumers, Internet tools such as these have become essential for managing their busy lives. Millions of consumers around the world spend many hours a day on the Internet. It's an essential part of their work life, and often their home or social life. For younger consumers especially, the online and "offline" worlds are seamless. They switch effortlessly from updating their MySpace page to sending text messages and doing research for school.

Windows Live is a promise by Microsoft to make these consumers' lives easier and more fruitful. Most know how to use the tools available to them. They may not be tech-savvy, but they're familiar enough with what they use. However, Internet services are a fragmented experience. Users often must sign in to one service, sign out, and sign in to another service as they navigate through their different service choices. As a result, consumers tend to take an *a la carte* approach to their favorite products. They use multiple brands of Internet services as opposed to building a relationship with one brand that can take them wherever they want to go on the web.

Windows Live offers the functional benefit of signing in once so that all of the customers' Internet services needs can be fulfilled without signing in and out multiple times. All their files can be accessed and shared quickly on a laptop, digital camera, and phone. The same is true for their professional and personal contacts, which can be continuously updated and integrated on all modalities.

However, these are functional benefits, and brands must have an emotional connection to their customers to sustain loyalty, premium pricing, and growth. As Mark McCallum stated in the offline world of Jack Daniel's®, "If your brand relevance is based on an emotional benefit, then you can thrive for generations, but if it's a functional benefit, you are only as good as the next invention." In the case of Windows Live, the "next invention" may be fabulous Internet services capabilities that provide customers with unprecedented flexibility and access to what's important to them; nevertheless, it's still a functional benefit.

We asked Peter Boland (now Global Brand Director for iShares at Barclays Global Investors) to speak with us about the challenges of capturing emotional equities with the Windows Live brand. We asked him about applying the insights-generation process to building brand equity with a consumer-centric view in Microsoft, a company that (like most technology companies) has traditionally had a product-centric orientation.

Peter Boland

Pete began his marketing apprenticeship at P&G, mastering the classic best practices of packaged-goods marketing in a rigorous and competitive context. He applied much of what he learned in international markets of varying sizes and development.

He transitioned from packaged goods to financial services with Visa International, where he expanded his global view and country-by-country channel and partner management experience, as well as immersing himself in another consumer category. He also worked in consulting, giving him the opportunity to objectively observe and advise on the application of marketing in fields ranging from server-based computing to manufacturing supply chains. At Microsoft, Pete helped create a great brand in a field noted less for its great branding work than for its technology feature wars.

Leading with Insights Is a Difficult Challenge for Technology Companies

Pete sees three reasons why technology companies have not historically built strong emotionally anchored brands founded on consumer and customer insights into the way that Mike Keyes and Mark McCallum described for Jack Daniel's:

➧ Technology companies just don't have an embedded heritage to synthesize and leverage consumer insights that drive businesses. So they tend to miss the opportunity for insights-led brand building.

"Although technologists have a difficult time with cross-category comparisons from software to consumer goods, I still think it can be instructive to take lessons from industry best practices and find the bridge to your own category. A great example is P&G's Bounty paper towels brand. The product is based on an engineering-created breakthrough (superb liquid absorbency performance). But what makes this engineering resonate is the brand's emotion-based consumer insight. Essentially, Bounty can contribute to a better relationship between a parent and child, obviously a highly desirable emotional benefit. When the child makes a spill, Bounty is strong enough to clean it up without fuss, so it's not a disaster. The relationship is not affected, and you're not mad at your kids. Bounty is the hero for delivering this benefit, and parents trust the brand to do so and therefore stay loyal. I've always thought this is a simple and striking example of taking a universal, meaningful insight about parenting and channeling it specifically to a product. The lesson for technology marketers in this example is that technological benefits must be articulated in the emotional context consumers understand. I know this sounds obvious, but for tech companies it's not so apparent. We tend to believe consumers love our technology rather than the benefit that accrues from it. This tendency manifests itself in naming architectures that are confusing and complex, and consumer advertising and messaging that's at best me-too, and at worst cold and cluttered. So in the Bounty case, consumer insight is the core of the brand story. But in technology-led companies, there's just little history of consumer insight being at the front end of the brand-building process."

➧ The industry has always been led by its engineers, not its marketers.

"My company, Microsoft, has the most talented engineers you will ever meet. They've been engineers throughout their schooling and their work experience, and they approach product management and product development from a scientific, engineering-based point of view. Obviously they get really excited about technical capabilities, and that's one reason why Microsoft technology is so absolutely brilliant. Having said that, it's hard for a company with this kind of engineering focus to take a consumer-first point of view. It's very difficult for them to have the mind-set of your average consumer, be it a grandmother in Frankfurt or a small-business owner in New Delhi or Buenos Aires. In my experience the engineers rarely appreciate the crowding-out effect that the bombardment of information has on the mind of consumers. I think they believe all consumers have time to consider their product and associated messaging in detail. Everything I hear from consumers—and I've probably listened to at least 400 over the past two years in focus groups and one-on-one discussions—is related to the desire for simplicity in their lives. Engineers and product marketers must be able to look at a brilliant cluster of technological features and think, 'I'm not sure if my friends or my mother would have any clue how to actually operate that.' That's not the case for engineers who live in a techno-centric world."

➧ Technology-centered companies tend to make it even more difficult for themselves to navigate via consumer insights because they don't have the same input materials as a marketing-centered company. They structure their market research to focus on technology performance data or statistical support for technology benefits.

"Technology companies drill down into the data about product usage, but not into its benefits. Generally they don't step back from the technology and ask the consumer, 'What does this feature do for you? How does it make you feel? How does it change your life?' These are the crucial questions. Engineers can advance along the product development chain with no benefit-based consumer insight at all, and especially without understanding emotionally based benefits.

"The risk is that such a process will miss the point of the emotional benefit that transcends utility—and generates love, loyalty, and premium pricing. A brand built in this environment can only be functional—and purely functional brands are not the way to become a brand leader in most categories.

"Fortunately for the company, this is becoming less and less the case at Microsoft. There's been a real shift in appreciation of the value of consumer insights. The marketers in the Windows Live group are highly aware that, as a challenger brand to entrenched winners in Internet services, such as Google, AOL, and Yahoo!, we really have to demonstrate our understanding of consumers and show them we're on their side. To do so successfully, we truly need to understand what being on their side really means, and that requires the insights that support such a deep level of understanding. You'll see in our communications that we're getting better. We have the right mind-set."

Can Technology Brands Have an Emotional Component?

Is it possible for technology companies to build emotional bonds with their consumers based on insights? Google answers that question. People love Google. Consumers are engaged, but not through advertising. Google has built real brand equity.

Brand equity is built on three activity streams: innovation, design, and the consumer experience. Google has succeeded in each of these activities.

- **Innovation:** Google has superior performance in search accuracy, as proven in performance tests.
- **Design:** Google has an extremely simple and easy-to-use interface. Design is the component that makes a brand relevant—that is, "right for me."
- **Consumer experience:** Google has a highly developed and fairly unique consumer engagement component. Every search query a customer enters is both a declaration of intent (telling Google what she needs and confessing that she can't meet that need without

Google) and a plea for help. There's a functional benefit in meeting this need; it's called "adaptive memory." In other words, you don't have to remember things if you know that Google will find everything for you. There is a clear emotional connection with Google. Google makes you feel competent without judging you.

So, Google has all the attributes of a strong brand—a promise to consumers, a functional benefit, an emotional benefit, reasons to believe it can deliver the benefit that are confirmed with every search, a consistent and excellent consumer experience, plus style and character. All of these elements are infused throughout the brand experience and reinforced at every touch point.

We've referred to Apple as another brand owner in the technology space that understands brand building. The Apple organization is congruent. Its employees understand the tone and style for the Apple brand. It recognizes that consumers receive an emotional benefit through the self-expression that Apple enables.

Consistent with this trend toward better brand building in the consumer software category, Pete Boland and his team helped lead Microsoft toward an improved brand-building future. He initiated the consumer insights generation process and focused the organization on the value chain to enhance consumer loyalty to Microsoft.

"Google and Apple are exceptions. Yahoo! may be another. But most technology companies, and I'd include the 'old' Microsoft in that group, do not have a history of a unified brand point of view or a history of building a brand that relays some sort of human emotional truth. Many engineers presume consumers are like them on the technology adoption curve; the engineers could benefit from the holistic insights generated to reach the target customer, and they need to learn how emotional connection adds value.

"By simply introducing the primacy of consumer insights in our development of the Windows Live brand, we have been able to make a lot of progress from this past."

New Insights for the Windows Live Brand of Internet Services

Simply initiating new learning can lead to a torrent of downstream marketing innovations.

"Our starting point was to conduct new consumer research and ethnography focusing on the *benefits* of Internet services to consumers. We were absolutely delighted with what we were able to reveal about consumer emotional involvement with Internet services. In the past we hadn't dug really deep enough to unearth emotional benefits; we'd tended to be satisfied with functional benefits such as 'It helps me get things done.' For Windows Live we deliberately dug deeper, using consumer-generated imagery to tell the story of the role of the Internet in people's lives. We uncovered three fundamental benefits of using the Internet. The three included the benefit of deepened relationships, enriched knowledge, and self-esteem.

"For example, the benefit of using e-mail and Instant Messenger is deeply emotional. It serves the fundamental human need to create and deepen relationships with family, friends, and strangers. It's absolutely seminal. The key learning for us centered on the role of e-mail and IM in eliciting deeper, more meaningful dialogue than face-to-face human contact usually has. That was new news to us. Consumers told us that they reveal their inner thoughts much more readily on e-mail, and especially on Instant Messenger, than any other media. Although that's a category benefit rather than a brand benefit, if our new brand does a better job than others in understanding and communicating that benefit, then we can begin to form our own emotional foundation for our brand's equity.

"Other Windows Live offerings have a similarly profound impact on consumers' lives, leading us to the realization that the brand could truly bolster consumers' self- esteem and confidence based on what quick, deep access to knowledge, and new, deeper relationships, can do for their careers and their personal life. It's inspiring to people. We were quickly able to uncover all this emotion that we could to tap into in order to differentiate Windows Live Services."

Using Insights to Create New Economic Value

Here's how Pete describes the new value that new insights can generate for a well-established brand like Windows from Microsoft:

"Mark McCallum from Brown-Forman talked about brand renovation and gave a superb overview of what's entailed. I use the term 'reignite' for the brand-building activities we've tackled in expanding the user value of the Windows brand to include Internet services here at Microsoft.

"Brand Evaluator studies show that the Windows brand is unrivaled in terms of brand *relevance* scores—far better than Google or any other category brand comparison. However, *perception* of the Windows brand has been fairly narrow; it is what users see when they switch their laptop on and off. Beyond that, broad brand knowledge is actually pretty limited.

"That's because Windows is an operating system that works in the background. Consumers don't think too hard or too deeply about it. There's not a great deal of emotional connection. Our task is to reignite the brand, in terms of driving deeper emotional connection, by stretching it into the Internet services space. We have only to rub a little of the Internet magic over the Windows brand, and it reignites.

"There are several very positive factors. While people are aware of the Windows brand, they do not know all of its product offerings, because it has been perceived in a very limited way. Once we dug deep enough to get a full understanding of the relevance of our brand, we uncovered very important attributes that the Windows brand stands for, including quality and genuineness. What was exciting is the potential strength consumers see in Windows' ability to make my PC and Internet applications work together seamlessly. It gets credit for that from consumers. But the rest of it is totally black space.

"We had to find a way to associate Windows with the new excitement and dynamic innovation of the Internet and to carefully and convincingly draw a new connection. We needed a deeper insight."

The Insight for Windows Live

An insight is a profound discovery about the motivations that drive human behavior. The job of marketing is to change what customers do (behavior) by changing how they think (attitudes). So, first we have to identify the behavior we want to change and then identify the attitude (or emotion, or motivation) that drives the behavior. Only then can we take intelligent action through marketing or product development.

For Windows Live, the core insight was built around observing fragmented consumer behavior. They use multiple services, often from multiple brands of service providers, and they act in an ad hoc, uncoordinated, unintegrated fashion. They experience the Internet as a cluster of component services. But the problem is that consumers often perceive that different applications do not work together, and users get a fragmented experience. They must do a lot of work on their own to navigate among different programs to try to make them all work together effectively.

Pete suggests that the act of identifying the insight unleashes the solution.

"With that behavioral insight, the Windows Live brand is able to respond to the user's need—and can do so uniquely—i.e., our brand is better qualified than any other—to build a service that makes everything on the Internet work together.

"The brand communications campaign builds on the functional benefit to reach for the higher-level emotional benefit: if all of the consumers' Internet services are working together as one, they will feel as though their whole world is working together. This feeling transcends the digital world. It is also about the way people can now interface with their professional and personal world as well. If you can make my Internet world come together, then I feel like the personal world I live in comes together. I feel confident and in control; I'm an achiever. Only Windows Live can deliver this benefit."

Using the Insights Process

Marketers can create opportunities for growth by first achieving a better understanding of their consumers than any competitor. Ask, "What do you understand about your consumers' needs that your competitors do not?"

Pete proved that this approach works for technology brands and services.

"That's how you win! In the consumer packaged-goods category, companies such as P&G find the unique marketing and messaging opportunities they are looking for in the emotional drivers of human behavior. We in the tech world have to learn to do the same.

"So, in our qualitative research to develop insights for Windows Live, we talked to consumers about their experience with the Internet, and we used imagery and analogy to get them to tell us how they feel about the benefits they receive from using the Internet. We explored how the Internet really enriches and changes people's lives. We didn't ask about the technology or how to use it; we just talked about what benefits they derived from the technology.

"When you use e-mail or Instant Messenger, what are you using it for? Who are you talking to? How does that change your life? How does that make you feel?"

Insights can cascade from high-level perspectives that can govern the development of major brands at a holistic level to detailed, localized, or product- and feature-specific perspectives for design, development, and differentiation.

"For example, another insight at a greater level of detail that we've identified is around the change in behavior that happens to people when they are using Instant Messenger or electronic communication. This new digital kind of communication is qualitatively different from traditional interpersonal communications like talking on the phone or talking face to face, and results in different behaviors. Consumers feel as though they can let their guard down and take some interpersonal communications risks they wouldn't normally take. As a result, many people who use these communications forms feel sufficiently liberated by the medium to communicate some things that they couldn't communicate before—like telling their mother that they had sex for the first time, as one respondent told us. The new permission that this form of electronic communication brings with it is something that's not inherent in features or technology, but is an abstract benefit that arises spontaneously from the medium."

Microsoft uses internal marketing, as shown in these pages from the Windows Live Brand Strategy book, to communicate the new insights about emotional benefits of software and Internet services (see Figure 10.1).

it's about relationships

Our consumers need to be able to easily connect with people. Gone are the days of getting up the nerve to place a phone call or losing touch with friends who moved out of your area code. Deep, thoughtful or emotional conversations you thought you could never have in person you can have online. The Internet enables everyone to be more approachable, but not if you can't keep up with ever-changing contact information or chat with people on different IM networks. People want to connect in meaningful ways.

Figure 10.1   Microsoft internal marketing.
From Microsoft internal brand book. Reproduced with permission.

Global Insights Drive Global Brands

A current debate in our global economy with global marketing is: Can there be truly global positioning, global solutions, and global brands? One simple approach is to ascertain whether there is a global insight. Suppose the definition of an insight is a deep understanding of target consumers and their behavior and the motivations behind that behavior. If you can identify an insight that applies globally, you can build a value proposition and a brand framework that apply globally. Mike Keyes, Global Managing Director for Jack Daniel's, suggests that the need to express individual independence through the choice of Jack Daniel's is one such global insight.

Peter Boland, who is a global marketer with experience in multiple industries, discusses this issue for Windows Live.

"On every continent we heard exactly the same thing. We heard consumers tell stories about how they were seeking to better their lives in every way they could. It's the universal human goal. And those consumers whom we might think of as the most Internet-savvy are using the Internet as a primary tool to achieve that universal human goal. Somebody we talked to in Madrid would tell us the same story we heard in Shanghai, London, and Los Angeles. The emotional intensity that people felt about the Internet is unlike anything I've ever worked on. It's transcendent. People talked about it being an open door to the world. Not so much about the product, but a state of being. It really was incredible— and truly global.

"So the end benefit of Internet services is what we call an enriched life and a unified world—your life enriched by deeper relationships and interpersonal confidence. That's an emotional benefit, based on a global emotional insight."

Summary

The power of the insights-centered approach to building brands and businesses is universal. It may have developed originally in consumer packaged goods, but its application is by no means restricted to that industry. It is the "source code" (to borrow a technology term) for understanding customers and creating strong, lasting bonds between customers and the products and services that meet their needs. Good outcomes cascade from the generation and adoption of customer insights. Customer loyalty shifts in favor of the business that demonstrates understanding, enabling the business to sustain premium prices, higher margins, and expanded lifetime values. Similarly, internal corporate behaviors shift as more energy is devoted to listening and understanding and to generating benefits as well as building features. This can be equally true in technology businesses as in more traditional consumer-goods categories. It's just as true in business-to-business as in business-to-consumer categories.

11

Marketing Knowledge Centers

- How can everyone in your company, in every country, on every brand and business, have access to the marketing wisdom, information, and lessons learned?
- How do you capture and share corporate knowledge?
- How can you accelerate the organizational and individual learning curve?

We have defined the new marketing as a process and a science rather than an ad hoc, communications-based art. The process and science of marketing are fueled by shared knowledge and information: knowledge of the customer, insights derived from this knowledge, information about the programs developed from these insights, and analysis of the results as measured by both customer response and enterprise revenue and profitability.

Most experienced marketers understand this. Nevertheless, senior managers tell us repeatedly they believe knowledge management has been one of the most neglected areas of the marketing discipline. Knowledge has been used to advance narrow agendas, such as the product manager's need to research the acceptance of a new feature, or Brand Manager A's need to achieve a performance edge over Brand Manager B. It hasn't been used to advance the broad agenda of generating shared insights and shared knowledge assets from which the entire enterprise can derive a return.

The Marketing Knowledge Center (MKC) is an important first step to enable an organization to systematically harness marketing knowledge to achieve growth. The MKC provides the organization with an immediate, sustainable competitive advantage: speed of learning. Accelerating the speed at which knowledge and information are shared within an organization is the equivalent of compounding interest on your investment in marketing capability by leading all marketing practitioners to the top of the learning curve quickly.

A marketer can save time and wasteful expenditures by understanding what has worked in other circumstances—or what did not work—and why, or by reusing templated knowledge for basic tasks. This knowledge enhancement enables marketers to accomplish their routine tasks quickly, freeing them and their teams to apply themselves to more important value-added activities.

Another advantage of the MKC is that the enterprise can capture the "corporate" memory and not rely solely on individuals as owners of the knowledge base. Companies can give their marketers the ability and tools to learn on the job, get all key data quickly, and hit the ground running on a new brand or assignment.

What Is a Marketing Knowledge Center?

An MKC is a comprehensive corporate digital library containing all the data needed for marketing to function at peak efficiency and effectiveness. An MKC is much more than a portal; it's a collection of all internal knowledge, best practices, and actions that have worked in the past. An MKC embraces best practices in marketing processes, data, analytics, and sophisticated modeling. You can also add enablers (guides, tips, and templates) to assist with marketing tasks. Enablers are tools to implement marketing tasks; they provide metrics to monitor the effectiveness of marketing activity. Because the typical MKC is deployed on a company's intranet, the data is available to all approved employees 24/7.

Creating an intuitively navigable MKC is the quickest and easiest way to begin your company's journey toward marketing excellence. It shifts knowledge from the erasable "write and rewrite" memory of an ever-changing human employee base to a permanent, growing, and synergistic corporate memory. Equally important, an MKC is a continuously visible symbol to your marketing personnel, proving that you are serious about giving them the tools to be more effective in their work. It provides a stream of insights on demand that they can tap into whenever they need knowledge to begin, strengthen, or complete an initiative.

An MKC Can Help Solve Problems

Few companies have a comprehensive shared knowledge base for marketing. The need for this capability might lead to small bands of professionals planning to create their own electronic library for their brand, region, or functional area. This narrow approach has several problems: no common standard across the company, no company-approved "best practices," no procedure for what's in or out, and no links to similar libraries in other areas.

See if these common conditions apply to your organization:

- Projects move slowly because a common process path does not exist.

- "The wheel" must be reinvented often, and mistakes are repeated frequently because corporate knowledge about what works and what does not has vanished with the relocation or resignation of key employees.

- New initiatives fail or succeed randomly because no proven repeatable development process is captured in an MKC. Different divisions or brands follow different recipes for new-product development.

- Investment dollars generate unreliable returns because what has worked in the past in a similar situation is lost to those who are new to the business.

- Needless searches, meetings, and debates squander human capital.

If your answer is "Sounds like us," you should consider an MKC.

What Is the Value of an MKC?

An MKC enables everyone in the company to share best thinking and best practices about its brands and business. These become readily available so that employees new to the company or brand can come up the learning curve rapidly regarding all aspects of the business. The MKC is even more important for global companies. Many regions outside the United States do not have good information, research, and metrics. The MKC provides easy access to the programs that have worked in other areas of the organization, and with a common understanding about customers and competitors.

By creating a comprehensive, contemporary MKC, companies can raise the effectiveness levels of their marketing processes and marketing investments. This effectiveness dividend pays out in several ways:

- It increases the likelihood of successful initiatives because marketers maintain a knowledge base of success models.
- It increases speed and agility, including faster time to market, because marketers collaborate around known processes and knowledge.
- It accelerates individual and collective learning, leading to a competitive advantage in speed to market.

Four Types of Marketing Knowledge

Marketers can more effectively implement knowledge management if the systems are developed to distinguish, collect, and disseminate differing types of knowledge (see Figure 11.1):

- **Best practices:** Processes and how-to tools. They are the least unique to any business and require infrequent updating.
- **Historic knowledge:** Past marketing and media plans, and creative, promotional, trade, and retail materials. These are somewhat unique to each business and require less-frequent updating.

- **Contextual knowledge:** Insights about consumers, channels, and competitors. These are unique to each business and require scheduled updating.
- **Transactional knowledge:** A strategy to tactical linkage with success models such as new-product launches. These are unique and require in-depth information and timely updates.

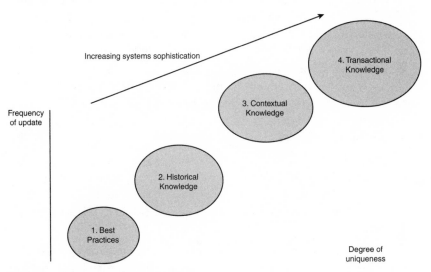

Figure 11.1   Four types of marketing knowledge.

These knowledge types provide the content areas. The next step is to understand what should be included in each of these areas (the taxonomy) as well as how to build a system that can be easily used by the marketing practitioners.

How to Best Manage Knowledge

A good MKC requires a holistic approach that focuses not only on optimal taxonomy and user interface, but also on the successful user adoption and system refinement to best meet user needs.

An "If you build it, they will come" approach doesn't work. Senior executives must transform the organizational culture through change management to achieve success. This should be practical and make sense for everyone involved.

We believe these three Rs for the MKC will help guide you:

- **Relevant:** Information is current for the market, business unit, and brand and is product-specific. The presentation shows a clear understanding of how users prefer to see the information displayed and what they will be looking for. There may be certain times or occasions when more users will be looking for more-specific information (such as annual planning). How will users quickly get to "their stuff"? If a user is seeking something that is specific to a region or market, business unit, brand, or product, don't make that person sift through everyone else's stuff.

- **Reliable:** Users will not tolerate a fishing expedition for information. You should include only what you can reliably deliver so that the user can anticipate what will be there and when. Users will look for content that is mutually exclusive and collectively exhaustive.

- **Ready:** Users should be able to quickly access the data through the use of well-thought-out search-and-filter functionality built into the system. Commit to publishing new content quickly so that users have a reason to keep coming back.

Treat your knowledge center like a product launch. Your users are your customers, so you should both market the MKC and measure its utility. Try to identify a single owner/champion who is responsible and accountable for its success, bolstered by senior management commitment and enthusiasm. The system should evolve to meet new user needs and maintain as open a system as possible. Users prefer that you use standard title structures and abstracts.

The following principles are key to minimizing user frustration and enabling the user to quickly and efficiently find what he or she is seeking:

- Conduct periodic evaluations: These should occur every six months or annually. They track usage (trial and repeat) and help identify priorities for system improvements.
- Set the evaluation's objectives: Identify usability issues to reduce frustration. Focus on knowledge gaps to be addressed. Understand areas of heavy traffic and activity so that you can build from what is most sought.

Use a combination of qualitative and quantitative data to gain depth and breadth of usage for a representative group of users. You should also sample both MKC users and nonusers so that you can understand why users visit the MKC and why nonusers do not.

Focus: Gillette Global Marketing Resource Center

The Gillette division of Procter & Gamble developed an advanced MKC in its Global Marketing Resource Center (GMRC). The GMRC has been operational since 2004 and serves about 900 marketing professionals in more than 100 markets. Its objectives are to enable and support knowledge management, capture and transfer best practices and processes across businesses and geographies, provide "just-in-time" training, and significantly enhance marketing effectiveness and efficiency.

Marci Sapers

We asked Marci Sapers, Gillette Vice President for Functional Excellence, to discuss her experience with the GMRC. She provides a candid assessment of the benefits as well as the difficulties of sustaining this effort.

Establish Clear Objectives

Investing scarce corporate resources in an MKC requires a shared commitment to a set of objectives that are sufficiently robust for a credible business case. From the outset, Gillette had very specific objectives for its MKC—the GMRC.

"In 2003 we developed our Global Marketing Resource Center to provide Gillette marketers with global access to business content 24/7 to improve their effectiveness and efficiency. We were looking to enable and support knowledge management, capture and transfer best practices and processes, and support the creation of a marketing culture and community. We believed we would increase productivity by reducing the amount of time people spent looking for existing information and knowledge and would allow our associates to leverage work that already existed."

Manage the MKC Launch as You Would Any Other Brand Launch

The CEO and top management endorsed the MKC. This facilitated the release of resources and the creation of a financial business case. As soon as funds were available, Marci's team was able to execute her idea of treating the launch of the MKC as you would the launch of any other brand or business. They used a rigorous approach in which they practiced customer centricity (the customers in this case were the company's marketers) and established customer needs.

"We built the GMRC using focus groups composed of people from our own marketing staff. We conducted several surveys and looked at what information our marketers used on a daily, monthly, and annual basis to do their jobs. Once the site was completed, we measured our marketing community to understand who went to the site and how much time they spent there. We conducted some quantitative surveys about user satisfaction. Based on these, we continued to enhance the site.

"We introduced the GMRC as a market event and treated this as a product launch. We created a lot of buzz around it, and I think that really helped. We introduced it with a big flash, inviting global marketers to Boston for the launch. We set up an Internet cafe and followed up with marketing material as if it were a new product. We continue to remind people both on how they can use it and the fact that we need them to contribute."

Observe Behavior Objectively and Be Prepared to Be Flexible in How You Collect and Share Knowledge

The purpose of the MKC is to disseminate knowledge. Therefore, it's necessary to add and subtract content based on its usage. It's also necessary to be flexible in data-collection methods, as Marci explains when she talks about the value of sharing knowledge about mistakes.

"As we measure the utility of the knowledge we share, we find, for example, that new-product launches have been the most popular area in the GMRC. Gillette has rolling launches. We do not launch in every market simultaneously, so we put together a launch center that can be used for pre-launch, launch, and post-launch information. Our marketers seem most excited about getting this kind of launch information. The launch promotions center, with toolkits for rolling launches, is very popular, too. Essentially, this knowledge falls under the heading of success models, and marketers are proud to submit them to the GMRC.

"We focused on the most important specific content areas and identified those priorities around key marketing deliverables for the year. For example, when marketing plans were being developed, we would send a specific communication to the knowledge-sharing partners, asking them to submit content related to their plan development and a copy of their final marketing plan. We would send them ongoing communications and take baby steps. For example: 'This month we are focusing on getting marketing plan information. And by the way, these are the gaps that we had for your group, and this is what we need from your group.' We develop many of these focused communications and spend a lot of effort to get what we needed.

"Mistakes can also have value. In fact, some pretty senior people have said to our organization that we want to learn from our mistakes, too. Sharing what's working and what hasn't worked are both important. It's a hard area to get people to submit context/concepts showing their mistakes. People often want to bury mistakes. As we built this knowledge center, we asked people to showcase their successes as well as their failures to help our organization avoid repeating failures. I can tell you that we didn't get a lot of the failures submitted.

"So, to populate our key learning sections—which summarize learnings, including mistakes, related to specific programs—we conduct one-on-one interviews to gain information on both success and failures, and from the interviews, we develop an executive overview. This approach was more successful than simply asking people to submit presentations or even overviews of programs that did not work."

Maintaining the Knowledge Center Requires an Ongoing Team Effort

Not only does the MKC require a rigorous and creative effort to design and launch, it also requires continuing commitment of resources and energy. Marci describes how she created the virtual team of marketers to submit content and how she maintains the level of enthusiasm.

"Developing knowledge centers is a lot of work; maintaining them also requires a lot of resources. You need to continually add fresh information and visuals to encourage people to come back on a consistent basis.

"There was a lot of management support to set up and maintain the site. We continually reported participation in submitting content as well as usage to senior management. Additionally, we identified a key contact in each work team from around the globe. Each of these 'knowledge-sharing partners' (people specifically responsible for evaluating or submitting content within each of the groups) included the submission of content as part of their performance objectives. This was very important, since people had accountability and were rewarded for providing content to update the site. Our ability to maintain the enthusiasm for people to keep on sharing was a challenge. We developed contests and recognition awards to encourage ongoing enthusiasm.

"Honestly, we don't have the same enthusiasm for document submissions that we had initially. We were on a roll, and we saw from the time we launched it to the time of the acquisition announcement by P&G, each month submissions were increasing.

"We hosted a 'Marketing Council,' which met regularly and included about 25 Gillette VPs of Marketing. During our meetings, we always had a 'showcase on performance' presentation. By showcasing performance of their groups in number and quality of knowledge submissions versus their peers, we created some incentive for them to motivate their groups to submit documents. We also presented them with site improvements to get their buy-in to our changes, as well as enlist their support to help communicate the updates to their groups.

"We are continuing to evaluate the content and taxonomy of the site and update it on a regular basis. We now have a lot of great documents in the GMRC, and recently selected new knowledge-sharing partners to continue the work of gathering current information."

Don't Let Technology Get in the Way of Effective Knowledge Sharing

One of the key elements of the MKC is that it is digital and uses the power of technology. It's available 24/7, searchable, flexible, easy to add and remove content, and highly expandable in the number of users who can participate. The technology should be tailored to the task; otherwise, it can get in the way as much as it helps.

"We spent a lot of time up front in surveys and questions, getting the taxonomy right. We had an advertising bucket, a media bucket, a marketing planning bucket, and a promotion bucket, with documents in each to support them. However, until people start using the site, you don't know exactly what they're looking for. Once the taxonomy was established, the technology we used to build the GMRC did not have enough flexibility to change. It took us a long time to get some of the enhancements that we needed based on what documents the users wanted to see, and how they used the site. One of the disappointments was the lack of flexibility in the technology to give some of the capabilities that we would like. It was very difficult and slow to change.

"We used legacy software and systems rather than a new software system identified and designed for what we wanted to achieve. This created ongoing difficulties. I was surprised how long it took us to make changes for a new idea or even to update how we presented some brand information."

How Do You Measure Success?

Marci's experience indicates that it's necessary to be flexible in defining the measures of success, and it takes a willingness to combine quantitative and qualitative measures. When you do so, interesting insights can emerge.

"There are multiple ways to measure success. You can measure success by the number of visitors and visits or by looking at the content and application of the information on the site. In our case, we identified a full range of general and specific measurements objectives, such as what percentage of the marketing population went online and how many times they visited the site. We also tracked content submissions by group and made several qualitative assessments of use and application.

"Honestly, it was hard for us to know how people were really using the site and how it improved their effectiveness and efficiency. However, from the informal feedback of comments and e-mail we received, we learned that the farther away marketers were from our global HQ in Boston, Massachusetts, the more they felt the site was helpful.

"I think measurement of effectiveness is still the million-dollar question: how to measure it? At our peak, 75% of our marketers were utilizing the site. The GMRC was used by a majority of our marketing professionals, or at least they were familiar with it. Almost two-thirds of our marketers visited the site multiple times per month at peak usage.

"So, we can measure who is going there, how long they are spending on the site, even what documents they are reviewing, but in terms of our ultimate goal of increasing efficiency and effectiveness of marketers' jobs, that is subjective and much harder for us to discern."

Marci's Lessons Learned

- Do a lot of preparation up front to understand user needs.

- Spend time not only identifying the knowledge and content that users need, but also designing the taxonomy of how it's arranged.

- Put the right incentives in place for marketers to contribute content.

- Understand that the new approach to knowledge sharing is a cultural change and, as such, it will take time to get marketers to participate.

- Continued effort is required to maintain both the quality of the knowledge-sharing site and the organization's enthusiasm for using it.

- Manage a community of knowledge-sharing partners, users, and senior management.

- Measurement is hard, but it repays your effort.

12

The New CMO

- Why must the CMO become a marketing technologist and integrate brand experience into enterprise operations?
- How can IT create greater brand value?
- How can IT build and leverage global B2B accounts?
- How can IT provide consumers with "benefits on demand"?

The Marketing and IT Functions Merge: Chief Marketing Officer

Chief Marketing Officer (CMO) is a relatively new title in the C-Suite. The definition and job content vary in different companies. There are no accepted industry standards.

We observe there is a correlation between the defined role of the CMO and the organization's perception of the role of marketing.

If we think of the range of CMO styles as a continuum, there are two anchor points:

- **Marketing activation CMOs** actually "do" marketing, commanding large budgets and leading large program development and executional teams who report directly to them. They often provide a sales support function. These CMOs focus on current-year execution of research/analytics/insight-gathering and reporting, and on current-year implementation of marketing communications (advertising, promotion, and public relations). Their role is typically to

- Drive revenue via marketing programs.
- Achieve both customer acquisition and customer retention.
- Build brand health through marketing communications. For the type of organization in which this CMO operates, this is often expressed as "brand awareness" generation.

- **Marketing capability-building CMOs** focus on building marketing capability rather than "doing" marketing. They sit at the center of the enterprise to design and build marketing capability so that it can be deployed in the business units that build brands. As part of a matrix organization, the CMOs lead via a high span of influence but a low span of control. They do not command large staffs or budgets. Their role is to
    - Develop best practices, processes, methods, and tools.
    - Identify the talent needs of the marketing function and make sure that the right talent is recruited, trained, and deployed to support the enterprise's growth needs.
    - Apply analytics and learning techniques to create insights and new success models that drive innovation.
    - Design and oversee the technology infrastructure to support marketing and make marketing operations more efficient.
    - Provide shared marketing services to business units where enterprise scale and the benefits of an enterprise standard can make a meaningful difference.

We observe that CMO capability building is the emerging trend. However, the true C-Suite recognition for marketing has not yet become prevalent. The typical duration of CMO tenure is two years or less, demonstrating that expectations for this role are either poorly defined or impossible to meet.

However, we believe more CMOs will continue to evolve toward capability building, and that capability building will subsume the activation role. The new CMO will build capability and exercise that capability in brand activation. How can this be achieved? By integrating the marketing process with marketing technology, enabling one CMO to play both the capability building role and the activation role.

We can call this future CMO a "marketer-technologist." Here's the rationale:

- The CMO must drive the enterprise's growth. He or she will do so in collaboration with the Chief Strategy Officer, the Chief Innovation Officer, and the heads of the business units and regions. More frequently, the CEO will turn to marketing to fuel and accelerate the engines of growth. The CMO therefore will take responsibility for the relationship with the customer—defined as the customer's attitudes (satisfaction, trust, and love, defined via brand equity scores) that drive high revenue and high-profit customer behavior (loyalty and repeat purchases over time, the willingness to buy new offerings from the brand and to pay premium prices).

- The drivers of customer attitude and customer behavior can usually be grouped into three key areas:

  - **Innovation:** Does the customer perceive that the brand continually delivers effective new solutions to his or her needs and is always on the leading edge of what's available in the category?

  - **Communication:** Does the brand communicate in ways that are relevant, at the right time and via the right medium— via e-mail, website interface, streaming video, podcasts, sponsored events, word-of-mouth recommendation, or any of the myriad digital and nondigital channels and vehicles that customers use?

  - **Brand experience:** Does the consumer, in the experience of consuming the product or service, perceive that the brand delivers what it promises? Does it consistently meet the expectations it creates? Does it consistently meet the customer's evolving needs?

- To deliver consistent customer experiences, the brand must be fully integrated into the enterprise's operating system. This includes every call center operator at his or her console, every shipping clerk entering data into the logistics system to ensure timely and accurate delivery, and every IT and operations employee who affects whether systems properly support brand performance.

- To an ever-increasing extent, this requires consistency and integration between the CMO and the IT system. The CMO must become a marketer-technologist and understand how technology can support the processes that enable brand building to succeed.

Increasingly, the CMO must be able to command the IT assets that can advance the breakthrough enterprise marketing management systems designed to maximize the productivity and effective use of brand assets.

Focus on Hyatt: Tom O'Toole

In some leadership companies in some industries, the marketer-technologist CMO is already in place. Tom O'Toole, Senior VP of Strategy and Systems for Global Hyatt Corporation, is one of the best role models for this leadership transformation. We asked him for his perspective.

Tom's professional background illustrates the transition from old to new marketing. He began his career as a research analyst at an advertising agency in the narrow field of communications research methodology. He worked at the Wyse Agency, moving up to managing director for the Stouffer Hotel Company account. Stouffer recruited Tom to direct its marketing; subsequently, Renaissance Hotels acquired Stouffer. Tom became VP of Marketing of the Americas for Renaissance. He was recruited by Hyatt Corporation in 1995, where he has pioneered merging brand strategy, marketing, and technology into a new CMO role.

Tom initially experienced the classic VP of Marketing function, focused on marketing communications. But his career path changed when he became director of the Central Reservation function at Hyatt, which is really the central nervous system of the company worldwide. In 2000, he assumed leadership of IT. Under Tom's direction, the CMO and CIO functions merged for the North America business. In April 2003, the Global Hyatt Corporation was formed, and this subsumed all the various operating companies. This includes 215 Hyatt hotels and resorts (more than 90,000 rooms) in 43 countries. This new Hyatt structure is responsible for all the operating companies and respective brands addressing the distribution chain between Hyatt Corporation and the client. In the hotel industry electronic distribution channels have a long history of being the critical link to the customer.

The travel industry as a whole, including the hotel industry, has for many years based its customer relationship on electronic distribution systems more than most other industries. The Sabre reservation system developed by the airline industry in the mid-1980s was one of the largest private telecommunications networks in the world. Electronic networks became the industry's basic operating infrastructure. Hotels have very accurate transaction data; the capability to maintain this data by individual customer enabled the hotel industry to become a leader in database marketing.

This technology leadership put the industry in a position to take advantage of the emergence of the Internet. Internet distribution has restructured the travel industry in many ways. Hyatt was already doing most of its business electronically and was well placed to leverage IT. Tom's challenge was to incorporate Internet distribution into the existing electronic distribution channels. So it is no accident that he came to be at the forefront of integrating IT into the core of the new CMO job function; the travel industry is the perfect laboratory to merge marketing and IT.

Here are Tom's views on the new role of the CMO; the merging of brand strategy, marketing, and IT; and some examples from the Global Hyatt Corporation of how these principles can be implemented now and in the future.

The IT Evolution in the Travel Industry

As Tom describes it, historically in the travel industry, marketing was just the brand communications and promotion function. It focused on marketing communication through mass-media advertising, with a special expertise in "frequent flyer" programs. Marketing had no connection to the revenue-generating function of the reservation center—it was an activity in a vacuum. Only when marketing became Internet-enabled could it escape its silo and reconnect with the rest of the enterprise functions.

"Here is a simple way to view this. Circa 2000, we started running a banner ad on Yahoo!. It was linked into our central reservation system for a promotion offer with a special rate and limited inventory of rooms attached to it. So in that example, one could ask, 'Is that marketing? Or is that management? Or is that central reservations?' Well, it's all three. The line crosses the conventional, functional definitions. By the late 1990s it became obvious that these were becoming arbitrary distinctions among the respective functions. Today if you were reading about business intelligence analytics, you could find it in a marketing publication or in an IT publication. The distinction ceases to exist."

It was the integrative dynamics of real-world business systems—not some theory or ideal—that drove the transition of the CMO job at Hyatt. The historic flash point was the development of branded Internet sites that could accept reservations. As soon as the brand started to generate tens of billions of dollars worth of business through high-tech communications, the synthesis became an imperative. IT and marketing together drive the traffic to the website, and IT and marketing together ensure that the entire customer experience is seamless through to the back end of operational delivery at the hotel location itself.

"When I was interviewing candidates for a Chief Technical Officer position a while ago, I would ask every candidate, 'In your company, where does brand strategy reside? Is it under marketing or under IT?' And the answers were about 50/50, which indicates to me that different companies hadn't really figured it out and were doing it different ways."

IT Can Create Greater Brand Value

Frequent guest programs have been around for a long time, entirely IT-enabled. These programs are cornerstones of Hyatt's brand equity because they affect the attitudes and loyal behavior of the most valuable customers. As befits a premium brand, Hyatt's most focused efforts are promotions directed at more affluent customers. Affluent customers are more demanding and are greater seekers of personalization. The relationship programs are maintained and executed through database management and database marketing. So customer relationship management (CRM) is about personalization and customization of the guest experience, knowing guest preferences and enabling their delivery through the property management system, which is the property's information infrastructure. True integration in marketing and IT really means that the property management system (technology-enabled operations) needs the functionality to deliver on the guest preferences that are captured by the CRM system (technology-enabled marketing).

The quality and capability of marketing-IT integration are directly related to the creation and enhancement of brand value. The advances in integration between CRM and the property management system deliver competitive advantage for Hyatt in the hotel industry.

"Several years ago we developed the capability for guests to identify specific interests that they had, or specific destinations that they're interested in, and to receive specific offers from us through our e-mail programs on Hyatt.com. The customers personalized our marketing to themselves. We held an advantage for a while, but the industry moves fast, and today this has become relatively typical for most hotel chains.

"So we have just now taken our capability to a new level. It is called e-concierge. The customer can now go online and do all the things they would normally do with the concierge at the hotel: book a restaurant reservation, reserve a tee-off golfing time, whatever it may be, and do so online before checking in. Now we combine that with a PDA (personal digital assistant) or a self-service kiosk that's in a lobby. The self-service kiosk has all the functionality that the behind-the-desk property management system has. So when we combine Internet self-service with a PDA, or a Wi-Fi-enabled device, there are actually a lot of cool things we can do to let our guests prearrange their settings and maximize the sense of customization that they feel. We've seen fast adoption of e-concierge services; our customers like them" (see Figure 12.1).

Figure 12.1   Hyatt's advertising campaign.
Provided with permission by Global Hyatt Corporation

Marketing-Technology Integration Drives Continuous Brand Growth

Tom leads a relentless drive for continuous improvement in the linking of marketing and operations through technology.

"I would say we have become advanced in linking marketing activities to include rate management, inventory management, as well as conventional marketing activities. We are linking those to operating and financial results through Hyperion—our enterprise, financial, tracking, and reporting system. This gives us a global, enterprise-wide platform that we can use to discern relationships between marketing expenditures, marketing activities, and operating performance and financial results.

"We have multiple brands: Park Hyatt, Grand Hyatt, Hyatt Regency, and so on. We can correlate marketing expenditure by brand to operating margin by brand, and revenue by brand—all the metrics one would want to look at by brand worldwide, both from a marketing and operating point of view. That is something that we couldn't do two years ago. So now we can use IT-enabled systems to guide brand strategy in real time."

IT Enables the Details of an Individual Customer's Experience

Tom ensures that the marketing-IT integration is driven by the principles of customer insights. One of those insights is that a hotel guest's perception of the customer experience can revolve around the tiniest detail. A lot of details done right add up to a good experience; a single detail done wrong can mar the perception of an entire hotel stay. For example, consider the new technology-enabled world of checking in online and customizing your preferences online and never having to go to the check-in desk in the lobby. How does the guest obtain his or her room key?

"A guest can actually check into the hotel now through an Internet terminal access or web-enabled PDA. We call it 'web check-in' (see Figure 12.2). And with the new self-service terminals, whose inner workings have come a long way, we now can easily and quickly dispense the key. The guest can go to the web, check in, come to the hotel, punch into the self-service terminal, it 'spits out' their key, and they're in. It has become very popular. The most basic measure when we introduce a new capability is, do guests use it? Both the web check-in and e-concierge usage are really ahead of our expectations."

Global B2B Account Relationships

A hotel chain's marketing task is simultaneously business-to-consumer (B2C)—enabling an optimum experience for the individual—and business-to-business (B2B)—enabling a global customer relationship with the largest corporations and their legions of traveling executives. Hyatt's marketing and sales automation systems for global accounts must scale to the largest customers as well as handle the needs of individuals. Hyatt's marketing must be geared to generate insights about these corporate customers' needs and then meet those needs superbly through the same principles of marketing-IT integration.

Tom gives an example of how the system must be enabled for the corporate customer experience.

"We do business with IBM, and they want to operate their corporate travel program through our hotels. Let's say they want to plan a conference meeting in Atlanta. We need a system in place to enable IBM to directly access the Hyatt in Atlanta. They can access the inventory and the rates of inventory and make a booking. The ability for an IBM sales manager in Germany to book a meeting or check for availability of meeting space in Atlanta is something important we can offer our global accounts.

"Similarly, the system provides the CRM data for us to manage the relationship. If we want to know how much business the account did with every other Hyatt hotel around the world, the same global account management system can monitor and present the data and the trends. This is one of the features we're in the process of putting into place right now. About half our sales in North America are groups and meetings; they are a mainstay of our business. So the system must serve both the individual guest and the global corporation."

Technology Drives Brand Differentiation and Premium Margins

Brand building in the hotel industry is becoming more challenging as it becomes more fundamental to compete and win a share of the lodging wallet. Brand owners are operating portfolios of brands. This requires expertise in customer segmentation and the tailoring of the customer experience for each of the target segments, while also managing premium pricing and enhancing margins. It's a tall order. But as Mark McCallum, Chief Brands Officer for Brown-Forman's spirits brand portfolio, explained in Chapter 9, "Growth Through Brand Portfolio and Risk Management," the sophisticated financial management of the brand portfolio is increasingly the job of the CMO. Tom O'Toole concurs:

"Brand differentiation is the most fundamental issue in our category, because it enables our top priority: enhance the brand premium. Ultimately, we're talking about innovations such as the e-concierge and the web check-in to really create some brand differentiation and, at least for as long as it's sustainable, a competitive advantage.

"Imagine when you go to the hotel reception desk and the desk staff is typing away behind the screen because they're checking in a large group; perhaps a line begins to form. It's a turnoff. Well, a couple of years ago we started working with a technology to put the property management system access on a handheld device. With that handheld device, we were able to move check-in away from the front desk. When a big group is checking in, rather than having them line up to the front desk, we can create a separate check-in space for them. It's all part of enhancing the brand experience and therefore the brand differentiation.

"Technology also enables us to create new and better brand experiences from scratch. We are introducing a new brand called Hyatt Place that will be our competitor in the suites category. We bought a chain of hotels named Merit Suites, and we're doing an extreme makeover to reemerge as Hyatt Place. We are designing this experience to be state of the art, maximizing the use of the technology to offer customer benefits while at the same time reducing operating costs. So the front desk has been designed from scratch to feature self-service terminals. The food-and-beverage in the lobby is all designed around a self-service point-of-sales system. This is the first time that one could design a hotel from scratch using the latest in digital media."

The Future of IT and Marketing

Tom sees a world—certainly in the hotel business, and more broadly in the travel industry—in which IT and marketing will become ever more interrelated and the customer experience will become ever more IT-enabled. Brand-differentiating features will be created and enabled using IT. The marketing and IT functions will move ever closer together.

To illustrate this thinking, consider distribution management and inventory management. Companies such as Hyatt are coming closer to real-time automated decision making concerning rate and inventory decisions across distribution channels. Tom explains:

"It is not a complicated technical undertaking; we're rapidly on the way there.

"Let's say you click on Hyatt.com and want to book a room for a Thursday in January in New York. But you only want a one-night stay, and somebody else books the hotel for a three-night stay through a different distribution channel. We have one rate, and we accept each of those bookings. Now how do we take into consideration your value as a customer? If one reservation is from a high-value Hyatt customer who gives us thousands of dollars in business each year and is booking a one-night stay, and the other is a new or potential customer who wants to book a three-night stay, which one does Hyatt take, and at what rate? How do we marry CRM with revenue management and distribution channel management? That is where we are headed; in terms of business processes it's a complex dynamic undertaking. But if we can figure it out from a process perspective, we can implement it from a technical perspective."

Figure 12.2   Hyatt Place self-service: high touch and high tech.
Provided with permission by Global Hyatt Corporation

IT Could Enable "Benefits on Demand" for Individual Customers

Hyatt management focuses on what they can offer their customers—particularly, recognition for their high-value, most loyal customers. It's a competitive and dynamic industry, and initiatives such as room upgrades are quickly matched by competitors. Customer-driven customization is the answer. What the customer wants is unique to him or her, and the hotel chain that can respond to those customer needs on demand will be viewed as unique.

Here is Tom's view:

"Why don't we just let people tell us? If IT could deliver to the general manager of a hotel the information about what this particular customer really wants—a nice-looking room, three bananas, an orange, and a bottle of water whenever he walks in, for example—the general manager would say, 'Sure, I can do that. That's easy. All you've got to do is just tell me.' So we have to build a systematic way to do that. Instead of us driving CRM from our side, why can't we let the customer drive it?

"Once we have this connection of Hyatt. com to the handheld device, to the check-in kiosk, and it's all connected into our systems, there're lots of cool things we can do."

How the CEO Should Think About Marketing

Obviously, much vision, competitive strategy, and capital investment are required to integrate marketing and IT to seamlessly link the customer interface to operations. Although a visionary and qualified CMO such as Tom O'Toole can provide capable leadership, he and the new band of marketer-technologists will need unwavering support from the boardroom and from the Chief Executive Officer.

The CMO must help educate the CEO to think differently about marketing capabilities. There is a critical difference between the "old way"—marketing as a communication function—and the "new way"—marketing as a business function.

"I think the communications function is where a lot of CEOs, perhaps even the majority, view marketing. The way that I look at marketing, it spans not just the conventional brand communication functions, but also really anything that joins our customers and us.

This view has some very, very consequential business outcomes. If you want to talk to a CEO about advertising, will they pay attention? Maybe—to a point. If you talk to them about rate premiums, you've got their attention. Why? Because this is how the new marketing translates directly into operating profit.

"Now, if I was going to talk to CMOs, I would tell them, 'You need to take on the business operations side and the IT infrastructure side of the customer relationship and revenue and profit generation equation. You can't just take on the traditional part, like research and communications. You have to be responsible for the data center and all the other subjects and challenges that go with it.' This calls for a much broader definition than ever before of the marketing role, of recruiting for marketing, of training, education and qualifications for marketing, and the entire career path for marketers."

The Hyatt Corporation is leading the industry in providing both customer value and internal operational congruence to deliver that value through the convergence of marketing and IT. Tom O'Toole is a pioneer who is showing the way for marketing to reengineer itself to sustain top-line growth in a very competitive industry.

PART **III**

How to Get It Done

13

Managing Information

- How does the marketing organization become agile when applying information to real-time decision-making?
- How can the marketing organization increase collaboration and continuous improvement both internally and externally to create value?
- How does technology capitalize on knowledge to increase top-line growth?
- What do you need to do to manage information and knowledge across all business functions?

You need a strategic imperative to make your organization capable of acquiring, processing, communicating, and applying new knowledge so that it can quickly introduce new solutions to customers. If you can accelerate the pace of learning, and the organization can generate new knowledge-processing capabilities as an ongoing activity, this results in capitalization of knowledge. Speed of learning is a sustainable competitive advantage—perhaps the only remaining competitive advantage. Building these processes into the business culture is the challenge of managing information effectively.

In the new paradigm of marketing-led growth, managing knowledge and information is transformed:

Old Marketing: What Information Used to Be	New Marketing: What Information Is Now
Delivered from an information owner to an information customer when ready	Streamed
Owned by information experts	A collaborative work of continuous improvement
Viewed as an output of an information-gathering process	An input into the insight- and marketing-development process

Streaming Marketing Information to Be Agile

Traditionally, marketing information has been delivered in a "lumpy" fashion. A research report is issued. It is thick and data-laden, with perhaps a few conclusions, and it is hard to digest and process into knowledge that's truly useful for the marketer. You are familiar with weekly sales reports or reports about usage and market penetration. These documents have limited utility because they are usually highly delayed and therefore are a lagging indicator of marketing performance. You just cannot respond in real market time.

Information must be timely for management information systems to be useful. It must arrive on a cycle that coincides with its application for a business purpose: use in product design decisions, new marketing communications programs, or decisions about how to provide better customer service.

Today, these decisions are made at a faster pace. Internet services can be developed rapidly and released to the web within weeks or even days. The software development cycle—under a system called agile development—is highly compressed, and feature decisions are often made or reviewed daily. Even such traditional products as cars and detergents require rapid response to marketplace results and changes.

As the pace of marketing development quickens, we need to reengineer the pace of marketing information. Consider it a stream of data that you can tap into at the appropriate moment. You can be confident that it is accurate and useful at that point in time, with continuous change reflecting real-time marketplace developments. So, each time you tap into it, the data reveals what has changed.

We have become accustomed to this real-time information delivery in stock market trading. Now it is available in marketing information systems.

One way to accomplish this is to structure the knowledge base into a series of buckets of predetermined utility. These buckets can then be filled from available information streams. These streams flow at different rates and fill the buckets at different points in time. But whenever a user consults the repository, it is as up to date—as full of the freshest information—as it can be.

The voice of the customer fulfills this example and may include

- Segmentation data
- Usage information
- Attitudinal information
- Ethnography studies
- Qualitative and quantitative survey data
- Customer service data from a call center or website

This data has different periodicity, and it can be arranged into predetermined buckets (see Figure 13.1):

- **Who:** The customer and potential customer for targeting. This bucket includes segmentation data, demographics, psychographics, population trend data, and any information that can be used for targeting.
- **What:** Behavior, including what products and services the target customer uses, in our category and adjacent or related categories, and what related behaviors we can observe and measure that are associated with the usage behavior.
- **Why:** Motivation and the reasons, both functional and emotional, why the customer behaves in the observed manner. The "what" and "why" buckets are the source of insights, the critical fuel cell of the marketing engine.

- **Where:** Channels and usage locations. Where does the purchase take place, and where does the consumption take place? What other locations or emerging channels might become more relevant in the future?

- **When:** The usage occasion and every piece of information associated with it. For consumer goods, we can determine if the occasion is solo or with friends and family; is it frequent or occasional? For services, is the usage emergency-based or regular? For business-to-business, when does the usage of the goods or services occur, and how does this affect purchase cycles?

- **How:** How the customer uses your products and services; how the consumer uses media and how you can reach the customer; and other methodologies of finding, buying, and using that the customer employs.

Figure 13.1   The who-what-why-where-when-how organization of marketing information.

We can construct a website or web-based knowledge service that is prebuilt to provide information in these buckets. We can then link it to information feeds that push the relevant data (that has been meta-tagged and appropriately identified) into the right bucket. Whenever information arrives, it can update the buckets and alert subscribers to any changed information. The information may come from a research study, a sales report, or a continuous web crawl. Analysts may be able to add commentaries and draw conclusions and label these as commentary distinct from the raw information.

Marketing professionals experience the data as a stream. If they are subscribers, a frequent set of alerts arrives in their in-box, announcing new information in one bucket or another. Clicking the link takes the user there. Whenever they are engaged with a software development or marketing communications development activity, they can go to the site for the latest information. This gives them all the knowledge of the field at the point in time they need it. All products and communications are informed with the latest possible information about the customer; therefore, they have the highest inherent marketplace value.

Collaboration and Continuous Improvement

With finite marketing information—produced as point-in-time reports such as sales and distribution by region—there were separate information producers and information consumers. Information producers were specialists such as market researchers, ethnographers, data scientists, and analysts. Information consumers received this data as a handoff. They processed it into knowledge used in marketing and new-product development plans and refinements to existing marketing activities.

These disconnected roles with unrelated data reports are an anachronism. The marketing community, in its drive to turn information and data into a knowledge stream that continuously feeds innovation and better communication, must become more focused on collaboration compared to information producer/consumer handoffs. A good parallel is Wikipedia, the collaborative online encyclopedia. Its organizing principle is that knowledge is the sum total of contributions from a wide range of sources and people. It might not be as formally packaged and organized as the venerable *Encyclopaedia Britannica*, but the information is more likely to be timely. It also reflects the knowledge management of a community of people with common interests.

The *marketing information exchange* we propose is not quite as open as Wikipedia. It is a collaboration of all stakeholders in a company's marketing community—researchers, ethnographers, brand managers, product planners, product developers, field sales, and sales planners. It starts with the who-what-where-when-why-how structure, into which information is streamed from many sources (see Figure 13.2). An individual or a selected group of insights leaders applies a filter to the incoming information stream to ask if this adds to what you already know.

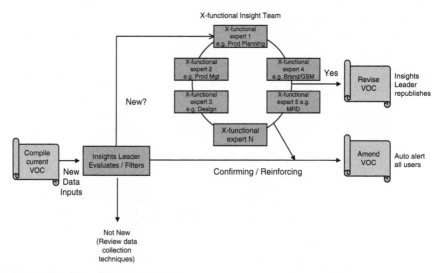

Figure 13.2 Voice of the consumer stream.

If the incoming data offers nothing new, it is rejected. A note is made to review collection techniques because knowledge processing resources are wasted if there is nothing new in the data. If the data is fresh and serves to confirm, reinforce, and update current insights, the knowledge repository (such as the voice of the consumer website) is updated. Also, subscribers are alerted to the new, updated information. If the data is genuinely new and can create new insights, the filtering team tags it and sends it to an expert insight team.

This team is not a panel of elitists handing down their judgment. Rather, it is an ad hoc group of cross-functional experts who have regular jobs in product development or planning or marketing communications. Because they are fully cognizant of current knowledge, they can look at new data and decide whether it offers new insight. They can call an "Insights Workshop" to creatively process the knowledge into a new, distilled insight. They can then publish the new insight and alert the entire community.

The community will then build on it, add to it, polish it, and give it depth and dimension from new perspectives and different geographies—in short, make it better and more useful.

Knowledge is a community asset and a community activity. It gains utility when it is shared and used by all.

Specifically, the benefits of this activity are

- Reducing the time required to achieve goals
- Eliminating redundancies
- Improving the ability to sense and respond to changing markets or service problems and opportunities

Knowledge and Information as Input

Data, Knowledge, Insights, and Innovation

Information and data can be transformed in a continuous stream of knowledge to help birth insights. In turn, insights drive ideas for innovations for new products, new communications campaigns, or new ways to serve the customer with a better experience. These innovations generate revenue growth. So information, in a series of state changes, becomes a revenue asset as an innovation.

Conventional information production is an output. Produce a great report, or a great dashboard, and you're finished. We propose that information is input to the value creation stream.

The information value stream is illustrated in Figure 13.3. Facts and observations are inputs at the base of a stream that generates ideas or theories to explain the observed customer behavior. The theories that best explain the behavior (or explain nonbehavior and suggest innovations that can change behavior) can be validated through testing. As soon as the validated theory—an insight—is at its highest point of development, it must be linked to action. Action is a new product or some other form of innovation that provides increased perceived value to the customer.

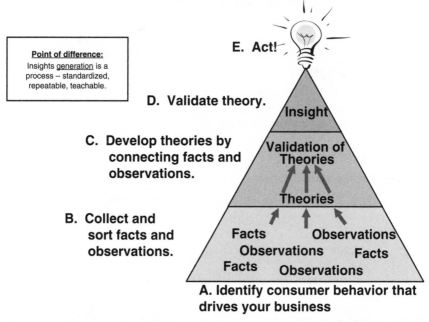

Point of difference:
Insights <u>generation</u> is a process – standardized, repeatable, teachable.

E. Act!

D. Validate theory.
Insight

C. Develop theories by connecting facts and observations.
Validation of Theories

Theories

B. Collect and sort facts and observations.
Facts   Observations
Observations   Facts
Facts   Observations

A. Identify consumer behavior that drives your business

Figure 13.3   How to generate insights.

The Role of Technology in Facilitating the Capitalization of Knowledge

Five processes use technology as a means and method to create knowledge for effective use in building businesses:

- Creation and discovery
- Access
- Speedy transfer
- Sharing
- Utilization

Creation and Discovery of Knowledge

We are all used to "Googling" for things we need to find out about. It's easy to forget that someone had to create the knowledge base for us to search in the first place. The Internet has lots of individuals and groups dedicated to creating knowledge that the rest of us can search for. It's one of the inefficiencies of corporations that it is much more difficult to do this inside the corporation, on the intranet rather than the Internet. No one is dedicated to knowledge creation in the corporation. It is necessary to create the corporate knowledge base that all users can contribute to and all can share. This is where technology can help: by creating one set of what the corporation knows. The knowledge base must also be able to absorb and present new data as it enters the corporation in a stream from sales data, user data, web crawls, and other flows.

Access

Often the corporation owns knowledge but users can't access it. The knowledge workers are denied access to the knowledge that they need to do their job most effectively. So the corporate knowledge base must be accessible to everyone who can use the knowledge to create value. It must be accessible via laptops, handhelds, and mobile phones on demand, using an effective internal search algorithm. When speed of learning is at stake, access is more important than security.

Speedy Transfer

Accelerating the speed of knowledge transfer from the field to product innovation is a winning strategy. Using the techniques of subscription, knowledge push, and linking names and titles to specific information sources, individuals and groups can become immediately aware of new information. In this way, technology can play a role in this transfer of knowledge. But human dynamics have an important role, too. The corporation must celebrate and reward those who transfer information via effective communication.

Sharing

Quantum leaps occur at intercepts of different knowledge bases and technologies. When medicine interacts with information technology in the analysis of the human genome, we can suddenly make incredible progress in solving medical problems.

All of this happens via sharing and connectivity between diverse bodies of knowledge.

The advances in the new marketing come from the same stimulus— the interaction of diverse approaches and disciplines. Marketers interact with scientists who address problems brought to them by market researchers. Chapter 7, "Open Innovation and New Product Development Through Communities of Practice," illustrates this.

Utilization

All this matters only if the knowledge and insights are used to create value through innovation to better meet customer needs, create better marketing communications, and do better marketing planning. Corporations must measure not the amount of their knowledge but the degree to which it creates growth in revenue streams. The return on information must be calculated. Otherwise, huge waste will occur in purchasing, or paying to collect, information that is never used— information on which there is no economic return.

Summary

- Knowledge management is a high-return investment for the innovative company.
- To match the pace of change, knowledge and information must be streamed rather than arriving in lumps.
- Knowledge must be accessible to all, in one place, representing "one truth."
- Information sharing is critical to creating value.
- Measure your return on information.

14

Metrics and Building the Culture of Accountability

● What should marketing be accountable for?

● How can we set objectives for a metrics program that are viewed as fair and valid?

● Can we measure how attitudes lead to purchase behavior?

Metrics are a thermometer, a simple but powerful diagnostic tool. No one was ever cured by a thermometer, and marketing will not be cured by metrics. The cure demands a rigorous end-to-end marketing process within which metrics play the same critical role they played in the total quality reformation of the supply side.

Every company, regardless of industry, needs to develop unique metrics, depending on what management expects marketing to deliver. We can start by understanding management's strategic expectations of marketing, and then measure that.

In successful marketing metrics programs, we set objectives:

1. Establish a framework to determine what works.
   ● Identify factors currently believed to drive business.
   ● Test the impact of these factors.
   ● Refine and improve the understanding of the business.

2. Provide a feedback mechanism for diagnosing and improving marketing performance.
   ● Improve marketing resource allocation.
   ● Establish explicit planning assumptions (targets).
   ● Compare the targets to actual performance.

3. Build focus and alignment across the organization.
   ✒ Create a consistent view of marketing's key drivers across the business.

Figure 14.1 illustrates the sequence of an end-to-end process in which metrics play a crucial role in engineering the marketing function to improve marketing effectiveness.

Figure 14.1   Metrics development processes.

The benefits of this approach are as follows:

- It aligns the marketing metrics with other corporate stakeholders in the larger accountability culture, thereby enhancing marketing's credibility within the company.
- It focuses the company on management's expectations for the marketing function.
- It ties marketing's metrics into the larger business planning process so that the company provides the resources that are required to meet the expectations embodied in the metrics.
- It mandates sharing of marketing function progress with the larger internal corporate stakeholder group, thereby providing visibility to marketing department contributions.

Using metrics developed from a subprocess such as this to knit together a larger end-to-end marketing process is one of the principal hallmarks of a best-practices marketing function.

The Culture of Accountability

Metrics, and the accountability they imply, create problems in all functions within all company cultures. Metrics and marketing is an especially volatile mixture because the marketing function has had few metrics in the past. Also, other metrically dense functions within the company (such as production management) are suspicious of the marketing department's sudden "foxhole" conversion to the discipline of metrics. Add the assumption within marketing itself that metrics are directly connected to personal compensation and career advancement, and you have a recipe for major cultural resistance.

Marketers must *want* to be measured; they must embrace accountability, or even the most artfully designed metrics program will ultimately fail.

The Attitude of Accountability

What most surprises us is the similarity of the cultural barriers between companies. Each company has similar hurdles to becoming accountable. Organizational alignment seems to always pop up. Corporate culture is the defining reason for success or failure.

Attitude drives everything. Perhaps you do not want to be held accountable because you do not trust your coworkers or you are concerned about how you will be evaluated and compensated. If so, the last thing you want is a metrics program or a marketing accountability initiative process.

Four conditions seem essential to creating the right culture:

- **Leadership:** Top management must be committed to a culture of accountability and provide resources to make it work.

- **Participation:** People want to be treated fairly. They become concerned when they see a process in which they are not given direction, yet the result will determine how they are evaluated, compensated, and promoted.

- **Process:** Metrics are the tool to measure whether a process is achieving the desired outcome. Metrics also provide diagnostics as to what parts of the process are working and what parts are not. Process is the prerequisite of objective and reliable metrics. Marketing has not been a process discipline, which is a big reason why it is not a metrics-dense discipline. Process must be in place.

- **Organizational alignment:** Process is, by definition, a workflow across multifunctional teams, in which several key stakeholders are represented. Marketing metrics systems must acknowledge this and align the various stakeholders, especially finance, market research, and the marketers themselves. If you can get groups aligned, you have a chance of winning. If it is a retail company, you may need store operations, merchandisers, and buyers to be involved as well. If it is a pharmaceutical company, you need to get the sales managers involved because so much of the marketing budget is spent on the sales force.

So the foundations of a successful metrics program are top management leadership, participation, a process, and a multifunctional team that has participated in creating the metrics and is aligned around their application. When the process is successful, everyone in the organization understands what the marketing expenditure delivers. You must have buy-in from all the critical functions in the company— understand what marketing contributes—and they can lend their perspective on interpreting the metrics. Figure 14.2 shows metrics maturity as a continuum and how you can evaluate where your organization is on the scale.

	Aware	Practicing	Established	Leading
Data	▶ Limited by type & function ▶ Unreliable time series ▶ Inchoate	▶ Available in limited, important areas ▶ Stable & consistent over time ▶ No integrated platform	▶ Broad spectrum time series data across geographies, customers & functions ▶ Some integration	▶ Integrated data platform across customers & expenditure types ▶ Capable of rapid cross functional analysis
Analytics & Metrics	▶ Accounting-oriented ▶ Backward-looking ▶ Inputs vs. outputs ▶ No framework ▶ Primitive analytics	▶ Limited mix modeling ▶ Oriented towards specific campaigns or expenditures ▶ No integration	▶ Some predictive 'success factors' identified ▶ Stable techniques ▶ Metrics tied to strategy	▶ Predictive & integrated ▶ Multiple tools, real-time response ▶ Continuous optimization capability
Culture	▶ Metrics is responsibility of finance ▶ Competing metrics by BU	▶ Management mandate ▶ Multi-functional team accepts responsibility ▶ Masses of measures reported upward	▶ Sophisticated dashboards encourage sharing ▶ Metrics broadly understood ▶ Professional metrics leadership	▶ Woven into every project & plan ▶ Understood, shared & lived ▶ Seen as desired capability
Process Embedment	▶ Pockets of projects ▶ No tie to annual process	▶ An appointed team ▶ Ad hoc process ▶ Annual review & modification	▶ Recognized high level ownership ▶ Stable, accepted, mature metrics ▶ Linked to planning	▶ Robust multi-functional process integrated into planning ▶ Metrics drive end-to-end marketing process

Most Organizations Are between "Aware" & "Practicing"

Source: Model adapted from DoD Metrics Review, May '04

Figure 14.2 Metrics maturity model.

For What Should Marketing Be Accountable?

We believe marketing should be accountable for something more fundamentally important than the short-term results of this year's marketing expenditures.

Figure 14.3 shows you the answer by looking beyond the annual income statement to shareholder value as measured by Wall Street. For most companies, total shareholder value can be deconstructed into three components:

▰ The corporation's "book value"—the hard assets such as buildings, capital goods, and cash.

▰ The adjusted net present value of this year's profits.

✒ The "difference" between those two amounts and the total value of the company. This is represented by share price multiplied by the number of shares outstanding. That "difference" for most companies turns out to be a fairly large number—something in the range of 35 to 50% of total shareholder value.

Brand Equity Driving Shareholder Value?

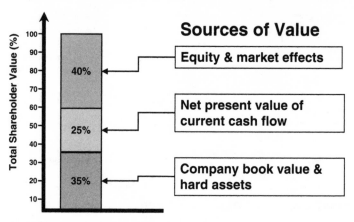

Figure 14.3   Brand equity drives market share.

Economists call that large, somewhat mysterious value by several names: intangible value, market effects, goodwill. Some call it brand equity because it represents the belief that investors have in the long-term profit-generating value of the brand behind the stock ticker symbol. Whatever you choose to call it, everyone agrees that *it* is tied to an expectation driven by a series of rational and emotional beliefs about the company's future performance. One might even suggest that it is related to the "carryover" a company gets in the absence of any short-term marketing expenditure. It's the loyalty the company has earned with a core group of customers who prefer the brand because of the perceived value from positive brand experiences, impressions, and promises.

We believe that brand loyalty drives financial results and is a function of brand equity and that brand equity is primarily a set of consumer attitudes toward functions or emotional benefits. So, the real trick is to identify brand equity attributes that drive contribution to preference. Measure them and develop a mathematical relationship between the movement of an attribute through marketing and the effect of that attribute on brand equity. Then translate that into market share.

Figure 14.3 shows how one marketer can prove that increases in brand equity are directly associated with increases in brand share. This marketer can deconstruct equity into various "contribution to preference" drivers and focus effort on the functional and attitudinal elements that are associated with increasing equity and share.

So when critics and colleagues demand that marketing be accountable, a fair retort is, "Accountable for what?"

The answer should be

Marketing is accountable for efficiently building long-term brand equity.

Measuring Marketing Results for ROI

Today we can measure marketing efficiency more precisely than ever before. A confluence of data, powerful hardware, and agile software enables credible measurement. Marketing professionals can no longer credibly claim that marketing expenditures cannot be measured. Evaluative metrics with relatively precise results from new marketing alternatives such as the Internet have fed management's desire to understand the relative efficiency of all marketing expenditures. Ignorance is no longer an effective defense. However, with more information available, it is harder to discern what information really matters. Metrics can provide the filter for management to determine what is important to know and what actions can be taken to improve ROI.

Marketers are beginning to understand that embracing accountability has its rewards as well as challenges. They can now optimize marketing expenditure choices across the entire spectrum. Instead of wondering which half of last year's expenditures were "wasted," marketers can determine how to make virtually all of next year's dollars count. What is needed is corporate conviction to create a culture of accountability backed by the money and resources for accountability initiatives to transform the organization.

Marketing should aggressively embrace the responsibility for the short-term ROI of its expenditures.

They should demand accountability for nurturing brand equity, the company's single most valuable asset.

Measuring marketing ROI can be done with significant accuracy, but it takes process, determination, and money. No magic bullet exists, but we now can measure upwards of 90% of what most companies spend on marketing. Yet, we have frequently seen corporate leaders who can be amazingly shortsighted. They annually spend tens of millions of dollars on marketing campaigns but do not budget several hundred thousand dollars to put the business processes, metrics, and technology in place. These metrics could effectively measure and fine-tune the marketing investment, with a probable 25% to 30% increase in effectiveness for the total marketing expenditure. If you could spend two cents to turn a dollar into $1.30, wouldn't you want that return?

Superior metrics do not in and of themselves deliver superior marketing results, which we define as robust brand equity leading to volume and profit growth.

The Correlation Between Attitudes and Behavior Has Been Proven

The marketing metrics conundrum is this: We know that attitudes drive behavior, but historically it has been extremely difficult to quantify the driving linkage. Marketers could track brand equity and market share over a long period and see a positive relationship. However, it is extremely difficult in the real world to measure both of those. The most important reason is the "Hawthorne Effect": People sometimes change their behavior when it is being observed and recorded. For example, in marketing panel studies, respondents may not make their normal brand or usage choices when they know they're being watched.

A.C. Nielsen consumer panels keep records of 125,000 purchasers. This enables Nielsen to cross-tab people's purchase habits across many product categories. Nielsen can then segment them by age, gender, race, household income, family size, and many other demographic categories. The bad news is that when you ask those people questions such as "Why do you shop at Wal-Mart?" or "How would you rate Tide on price or cleaning effectiveness?" you could start altering those people's behavior and destroy the value of the behavior panel. Therefore, Nielsen does not allow clients to ask attitude questions of their panel participants.

Kimberly-Clark found a way to get around this. It approached Nielsen to develop a different data source and create another panel that mirrored the demographics of the basic Nielsen household panel.

Kimberly-Clark then asked this mirror-matched panel about attributes so that it could understand the relationship between attitudes and behavior. Thus, the Kimberly-Clark study proved that brand loyalty drives market share, and brand loyalty is a response to functional and emotional attributes.

How We Can Track Marketing's Effect on Attitudes and Behavior

In the pharmaceutical industry, data gathering and analysis are facilitated by the fact that all doctors have a unique license number. This number goes on every prescription. So, the pharmaceutical industry has a perfect behavioral record. We can ask about doctors' attitudes before, during, and after marketing activity and match their attitudes to the behavior of prescribing certain drugs.

Working with the pharmaceutical industry, we have been able to develop what no one else in marketing has: a perfect closed-loop system that matches attitudes and behavior down to the level of individual attributes. We can identify for each branded pharmaceutical product the various attributes, either functional or emotional, that drive doctors to prescribe a drug. First we focus on moving a certain attribute (such as prescribing this drug improves the doctor's relationship with his or her patient, which is an emotional benefit for the doctor). Then we know with mathematical reliability that increasing that particular attribute, or moving the brand's ownership of that attribute, would improve the brand's market share. And we can isolate which part of the marketing mix is working to what effect on the doctor.

New Technologies for Marketing Accountability

A measurement company called Integration® (A Marketing & Communications Company) uses technology and new methods to crack this problem. It has developed a methodology to measure customer engagement from the many intervention choices marketers have to engage the customer. The company can prove mathematically that increases in engagement lead directly to increases in revenue and market share.

Integration® asks customers to identify all the ways in which they receive information about a brand, such as word of mouth, electronic mass media, the Internet, trade shows, and sales visits. Then it asks customers which of these sources provide the best information, such as which source they enjoyed receiving the information from the most, or which source had the most influence on them. From this data, Integration has developed an algorithm to derive a metric it calls the *contact clout factor*. It ranks by category the most important ways of engaging the customer.

Let's take the auto category as an example. In the automotive industry, marketers can reach their consumers and influence them using TV, print, or outdoor advertising; websites; car enthusiast magazines; and showrooms with salespeople.

Integration's algorithm can identify that the contact most correlated to a sale of a sports car is a test drive, the second is a nonadvertising endorsement in a car enthusiast magazine, and the third is a visit to the manufacturer's website.

The Integration system goes further to develop a mathematical formula called a "brand experience" point system. A brand experience point is a weighted average of how many times a customer or prospect has been "contacted" by a particular marketing message and its importance to the customer's decision-making. As soon as the common currency of brand experience points is established, it is simple to calculate brand experience shares—your brand's share of all the important contacts in the marketplace. This share measure covers all the key brands and all the key customer contact points in the category. Marketers can measure the changes over time in the brand experience shares and see how this correlates to the share of revenues in the category. This common currency of brand experience points and brand experience shares can be applied to any country or category. Marketers can now know the relative importance of individual channels (TV, showroom, website, billboard) to their sales in any country and any category. They can also calculate their return on brand experience, as illustrated in Figure 14.4.

Return on Brand Experience

The Return in Brand Experience – defined as the change on BES
over the change in total marcom costs – should always stays positive.

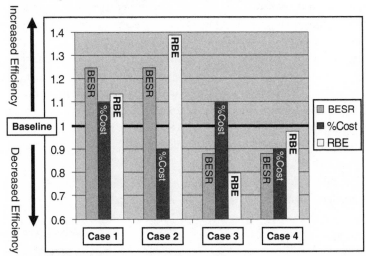

Prepared by Integration for Microsoft • June 07

Figure 14.4   Return on brand experience.
Provided with permission by Integration

Putting the New Marketing Accountability to Work

A large pharmaceutical company has been applying quarterly measurements of the effect of different marketing contacts and messages on doctors' prescribing behavior. This enables mid-course corrections to the contacts (advertising messages, sales calls, seminars); the adjustments are identified in the analytical model. We can ask, "How much did we spend for each intervention, and what was the ROI for peer-to-peer programs, compared to web conferences with doctors, compared to face-to-face meetings?" This directly links changes that have occurred with a specific attitude and the relative movement in terms of behavior (the doctor's prescription-writing behavior) associated with a specific intervention. It gives brand managers an unparalleled ability to constantly improve their message and the weight they put behind channel intervention (retailing, TV, print, Internet).

Influence Each Touch Point to Improve ROI

Metrics can also be useful to help us understand where in the customer decision-making process we can affect positive attitude and behavior change, thereby transforming marketing to a much more selective activity.

Figure 14.5 illustrates the purchase funnel or "leakage" model for each step in the decision-making process for a patient in the pharmaceutical industry. It also shows how each step reduces the potential number of individuals who will actually purchase and use the product. The marketer can influence the movement at each step in the transaction model and measure the marketing efficacy.

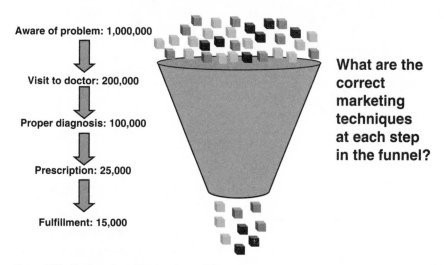

Aware of problem: 1,000,000

Visit to doctor: 200,000

Proper diagnosis: 100,000

Prescription: 25,000

Fulfillment: 15,000

What are the correct marketing techniques at each step in the funnel?

Figure 14.5   Purchase funnel/transaction model.

This model applies equally well to considered purchase categories such as automobiles and insurance. The decision of whether to purchase, what to purchase, and where and how has several steps.

It starts with need identification: "Am I even aware that something is wrong with me?" One of the problems with many diseases is that individuals do not even know they have it, such as cancer or ADD, or even high cholesterol. So the first step in such a case is to alert people to potential symptoms or other reasons to believe they may have the disease. The medical industry knows what percentage of the public is likely to have the disease, but individuals have to come forward and be diagnosed.

The next issue is, "I may be aware that I have the disease, but I need to decide if I want to do anything about it." People may say, "I have a rash. No big deal. I don't care. I'm OK." Or they may say, "I'll do something about it. I'll buy an off-the-shelf remedy." Or they say, "I need to go to the doctor." Then they decide to make an appointment.

After they go to the doctor, the next issue is, do they get the right diagnosis? If they do, perhaps the doctor says, "Let's just alter your eating and lifestyle habits." If the doctor does prescribe a drug, it might not be one made by this pharmaceutical company.

After the doctor prescribes a drug—hands the patient a prescription—does the patient actually get the prescription filled? A large percentage of prescriptions are never filled. There are many reasons: laziness, a dislike of medicines, or the person wants to see if he will get better without taking the medication.

Another issue is when he gets the prescription filled but doesn't take the medication.

The last issue occurs when he takes the drug but it doesn't do any good. Or it seems to heal him right way, so he never uses it again, and the rest of the medication sits on the shelf. Compliance and persistence generally are poor. So a medication that may address a chronic condition, and is prescribed for life, may be used for four months, and then the person decides to stop taking it.

Do any of these behaviors sound familiar? I bet they do.

What happens is that at various stages in the funnel, a fair number of people drop out; they decide against your brand or seek different treatments. So, the question for the marketer is, "What do I have to do in each phase of the funnel to improve the retention numbers?" In some cases, you tell people they have a disease and that they can do something about it. A good example is high cholesterol. Many individuals believe that if they look and feel good, there is no need for a cholesterol check. But suppose that you tell them that even the most healthy-looking individuals with good eating and exercise habits might have high cholesterol, which could impair their future health. The recipient of the information might be encouraged to get a checkup and, if necessary, begin treatment. The advertising for treating erectile dysfunction has become a ubiquitous example of alerting people to a common condition and telling them that remedies are available.

The point is that a marketer may choose different interventions, for different levels of the funnel, with different effects and different ROIs.

A sound marketing process combined with a well-designed metrics program will identify the right interventions at the right points on the funnel, with the highest marketing ROI.

Summary

- Marketing has reached a maturity level as a discipline that allows objective quantitative management via a system of metrics.
- The first prerequisites for developing accountability are cultural—leadership and organizational alignment to overcome resistance barriers.
- Customer attitudes drive customer behavior, and metrics exist to quantify this link.
- After quantification, you can refine the use of metrics to select and refine the right marketing interventions by using tools such as the market contact audit and the transaction funnel.

15

Communities of Practice for Consumer Connection and Open Innovation

- How can communities of practice improve internal and external communications?
- Can communities of practice improve product development and speed to market?
- Why is a corporate culture change necessary to make communities of practice effective?
- Can communities of practice facilitate the organizational culture change necessary for rapid innovation?

We have proposed that a different partnership with the consumer is essential to marketing success. One of the most exciting emerging processes to enable this transformation is the development of communities of practice (COPs); however, business management must adopt a different mind-set to make COPs work. In addition to enhancing the relationship with the consumer, COPs can be applied to improve cross-functional teams within a company as well as create value networks with external resources.

In this knowledge era, technology has contributed to rapid change. Customers now demand products and service capabilities that few organizations can speedily develop, produce, distribute, and service independently. Value-creation networks, such as those we profiled in the

Procter & Gamble Connect and Develop program, provide new organizational values, capabilities, and structures to support the constant innovation imperative demanded by consumers. These networks are a prime example of COPs serving as a constellation of expanded capabilities to augment the vertical staff organization.

Here are guidelines that enable linkage among all employees from different functions and markets as well as a real-time partnership with consumers:

- Innovation is constant and supported with resources.
- Insights are the basis for any initiative.
- A dialogue drives the development of capabilities.
- Learning and feedback are part of the marketing process.
- Collaboration improves capabilities.
- Technology, process, and the application of metrics improve our agility.

Naturally, any organization that adopts these principles needs to encourage collaboration to support this business model. The new rules change the corporate culture into a different organization.

Larry Huston, P&G VP of Innovation, provides a useful distinction between communities of practitioners and COPs. *Communities of practitioners*, such as trade groups or referral networks, have support and perhaps education, but the focus is on practice development of the members. True COPs share methods and solutions that transcend the interests of the individual practice. In a sense, wikis are a good reference for the COP model because they build on collective wisdom and experience.

Larry defined COP and discussed with us how COPs work at P&G.

Larry Huston
COP Defined

"To have an effective COP, you have to have a mission and an output you are really trying to drive. COP is all about creating results in such a way that the best learning and skills of a bunch of like-minded people can be transferred amongst each other toward some end result. So at P&G, the people who sit in the Colloid

Chemistry (how particles stay in suspended solution) COP will work with outside experts. If someone is formulating shampoo products or liquid Tide (both of these involve chemistry and solution), they have a common agenda.

"The bottom-line objective at P&G is to create superior products that consumers are going to love. And if you are involved with the Colloid Chemistry COP, you are sharing amongst each other the best way to do that, whatever business you are in. So for me, COPs are really focused on generating shareholder value, where learning of skills can be applied, thereby transferring learning among each other.

"Best communities are not about rules at all, but sharing what works and letting the things that work take off by themselves. At P&G we developed tools and infrastructure to engage people in Connect and Develop. People in the business units, who found cheaper, better ways, improved upon our processes. Some of the things we used early on were dropped by the wayside, since the people in the field could adapt, learn, and find better ways to do it. Part of the challenge for companies like Nine Sigma, InnoCentive, and YourEncore (innovation networking companies via the Internet) is to stay at the leading edge of COP with what people out in the field and companies are doing, and re-create their networking processes, so that they are at the leading edge of innovation. We are seeing that the costs are coming down with better ways and technology tools. My job is to find what is working, try and standardize that, and move it quickly across the whole organization.

"It is becoming more difficult for me to create the buffet of tools and say here it is every year. Our strategy is shifting now toward when you get 70 creative people out there, with a huge global ecosystem of suppliers and things available, is to pick the winners and to move them really fast, and be more learning-based; it is much more opportunistic.

"We are very much a learning culture. P&G management values the quest for new ways and to reinvent the company. That has always been a part of our DNA. Having a learning strategy, a systematic set of tools and capabilities. We figure out what is working and redeploy them really quickly to an area that we need to improve.

"If we could get all of P&G up to speed the same way as our innovation operation, the company would be even more successful. There are always some parts of the organization that are ahead of the other parts. There are mechanisms in place that help us to accelerate learning, and COPs help us to do that."

COP leverages technology so that you can be ahead of the curve for change rather than lag behind. Then give people the time, attention, and resources so they can work together to solve problems. This takes knowledge and collaboration, facilitated through technology, to create value. Value, rapidly developed to improve product and service capabilities, translates into increased ROI.

Partnership with the Consumer

Customers will have greater loyalty to an organization that enables them to enhance their own capabilities, thereby enhancing the relationship between the customer and the organization. The organization must implement a strategy in which the following occurs:

- Employees are encouraged to learn and increase their own capabilities.
- Increased capabilities are used to bring new solutions to the marketplace.
- The organization works with customers to improve their own capabilities to effectively utilize the organization's solutions.
- Customers become more knowledgeable and self-sufficient.

Consider the online systems in Amazon, eBay, and Dell, which enable the customer to become better equipped to make the company work for them. The interaction of these companies with their customers increases individual and organizational capabilities.

Technology is the conduit for this knowledge network; it is the pipeline through which knowledge flows throughout the organization.

The Power of Cross-Functional Teams and COPs

More companies now recognize the power of cross-functional teams. Consider this all-too-familiar scenario:

Traditionally, the contact point between the manufacturer and the retailer was a salesperson for a buyer. This was like two triangles with apexes touching. The salesperson had to do a lot of work that he was not qualified to do, such as answer the question, "Where's the truck?"

Salespeople spent half their time on logistics and resolving billing questions.

Companies such as P&G reversed the triangles so that the logistics people interact with their counterparts to locate the trucks and the finance people interact with their counterparts to resolve discrepancies in billing.

In addition, manufacturers provide real marketing benefit to the retailer, whose marketing had been historically underdeveloped, supplying it with information about the consumer. Conversely, the retailer could supply the manufacturer with information about the consumers' habits in the store. This is the power of cross-functional teams between organizations.

If multifunctional teams provide the power of breadth of information and knowledge, COPs provide the depth of knowledge within a specific discipline by having professionals collaborate, even if they work for competing companies.

COPs enhance the momentum in knowledge transfer. Often, the work that someone else is doing answers the questions in different areas of inquiry, speeding up getting to a solution. One engineer can provide answers to others in solving a technology question. On a COP site for e-learning, an HR person in the U.K. may suggest a report or case study to a marketing executive from a different company and industry located in California.

Increasing the speed of knowledge acquisition is a powerful competitive advantage. Therefore, the organization's ability to acquire, process, and apply new knowledge is a key factor in introducing new solutions to customers.

Mike Keyes, the Global Managing Director for Jack Daniel's®, uses COP to improve the marketing efforts of his global marketing team. They share best practices and ideas to improve specific marketing programs such as the mobile "Jack Daniel's experience." Another example of COP improving ROI is the way Jack Daniel's European marketing management has been able to improve its rock concert event sponsorship program in Europe through consolidation. Mike discussed with us how COP has benefited Jack Daniel's global marketing efforts.

Mike Keyes
Communities of Practice: Taking Lynchburg on the Road

"We have always believed that the town of Lynchburg, Tennessee is one of the reasons Jack Daniel's® is really special. Sammy Gully, one of our tour guides, says, "If you give me a whiskey drinker for a day in the Jack Daniel's hollow, I will give you a Jack Daniel's drinker for life." We have about 250,000 visitors to Lynchburg a year, but it is hard for people in Australia or most anyone to visit Lynchburg. So we try to bring the story of Lynchburg to the people. We do it through advertising, and the last ten years we've done it through the web, but now we have actually built a mobile experience, and we've taken some of the character from Lynchburg that makes our brand so special, and we have created a state-of-the-art mobile experience. We display at rodeos, NASCAR races, motorcycle rallies, and industry events. We send our tour guides from Jack Daniel's, so people at these events get our branded experience.

"Now our Australian counterparts discussed with us how to improve it. In the last two months the Australians have created their own Jack Daniel's experience, and it travels all over Australia for sponsored events there. It is a better version of the U.S. branded experience because they had the benefit of learning from us. One of the lessons from the States was that it took too long to construct and dismantle, so we were not getting enough display days.

"They partnered with MAC trucks in Australia, a good fit because MAC is a brand with similar core masculine attributes as Jack Daniel's, and they built this hydraulic trailer. Instead of three days for setup and breakdown, they just push a button and the walls expand. So, the next Jack Daniel's experience we make for China or Europe will take that learning and continue to expand on that.

"Another example of COP is in our global cultivation of the relationship to the rock music industry. Our marketers have capitalized on that through promotions in their diverse markets: the U.K., France, Greece, South Africa, China, and, of course, here in the United States. Our global team explored lessons learned. One practical application from this is our consolidation of programs in Europe, so now all of Europe is tied to the same programs compared with having seven different programs in Europe. They now put their effort behind one major themed event located in a different European market every year. This is a good example of applying benchmarking to increase the bang for the buck through the use of the COP for concert events."

Building a Value Network

Technology makes transactions within and between organizations cheaper and faster. So, many participants can create new value networks, with each organization or component in the value network contributing its expertise. These value networks are replacing value creation based on an exclusively vertical integration within the organization. So, external partners bring together their expertise, creating a network, with each contributing iteratively in their particular area.

The organization can thrive, rather than merely cope, with the rapid changes in the market environment. The network model (organizations partnering to create an integrated solution for a customer) then becomes a strategic resource, in addition to improving organizational productivity. It helps facilitate the organizational cultural change necessary to create the purposeful connectedness, so a collaborative infrastructure can be developed. Collaboration in an open environment is contagious. Once infected, most good professionals can unleash their creativity to move the business ahead in ways that cannot be foreseen.

It is like the Rosetta Stone phenomenon. In the Napoleonic era, the Rosetta Stone was deciphered in Egypt. One guy has the top half in hieroglyphics, and someone else has the bottom half in Greek. Put the two together, and you can translate the hieroglyphics and understand a whole language. With COP, a similar process is now accelerated and ubiquitous through the global linkage provided by the Internet.

Preserve Peasant Wisdom, Yet Break Down Walls

Another use for COPs is to preserve practical knowledge or "peasant wisdom"—ingrained knowledge within the organization. Some organizations are on the cusp of losing an enormous amount of peasant wisdom from sales and marketing people who are baby boomers about to retire. COPs provide a vehicle to transfer the experience and knowledge of older people to the newer executives. It may also be to counsel and help them not to do things that may be impractical. "We tried that several years ago. It didn't work, and here's why. Don't go down that path."

But COPs also break down the walls of the organizational culture so that people can question their mind-sets about the business and change the model. One example provided by Mike Keyes is Jack Daniel's recognition that its advertising portrayal of rural simplicity, which is perceived as a virtue in a frenetic urban lifestyle, may not work in Eastern Europe. There, the countryside is too close to reality to be perceived as idyllic relaxation. Brown-Forman executives in Tennessee modified their globalization effort in advertising by listening to their Eastern European regional managers, and HQ opened its mind-set to the market reality.

Mike Keyes
Rural Images

"Our Lynchburg-based messaging has to be balanced with the drinkers' world messaging. We are doing very well in Eastern Europe right now. We send our Lynchburg Southern tour guides. Many of them are middle-aged, in overalls and straw hats; that's how they dress. But in some markets that rural message may hit too close to home."

The More Knowledge You Have, the More You Realize How Much More You Need to Know

Picture knowledge as an area of a circle of light on a desktop in a dark room. We know the size of the spot of light, but we do not know the circumference of the room beyond the light. As the area of light increases, the circumference increases. COPs help management know what they don't know. IWIK (I wish I knew) can identify what they don't know and focus on attaining that knowledge. One of the major benefits of a COP is figuring out what we don't know.

Summary

Communities of practice can do the following:

- Change the corporate culture to become more collaborative.
- Speed up knowledge transfer.
- Leverage technology to stay ahead of the curve for change.
- Improve your relationship with the consumer.
- Utilize industry knowledge and improve cross-functional teamwork.
- Collaborate through a value network to create better products.
- Preserve and transfer accumulated wisdom and adapt to a global marketplace.
- Help you recognize what you do not know.

16

Empowering Change
from the Top Down

- How can CEOs manage the transformation of the marketing function?
- How does the CEO defy growth boundaries?
- How does the CEO encourage organizational skill sets for developing and applying insights?
- How can you apply positive risk management to convert insights into innovations quickly?

Now you can see that marketing is the holistic single-threaded system for driving growth from the starting point of insights through to the marketplace execution of new ideas, new products, new messages, and new customer experiences. Clearly, this definition of marketing is not limited to a department, a function, or a group of specialists. It's a core capability of the enterprise that must be designed, built, and deployed. The magnitude of change required cannot bubble up from the bottom; the sustained change in processes, methods, culture, and thinking requires leadership from the very top.

The words "marketing" and "CEO" are often not closely associated. Most CEOs did not get to their position through the marketing department. Their experiences and skill sets usually are based in finance or operations. Many CEOs may be suspicious or skeptical of marketing because, in their historical experience, marketing's promises have not been fulfilled, risks and rewards have not been adequately balanced, or process and measurement have not been balanced. Many CEOs are not comfortable enough to manage marketing, in contrast to their total command of the rest of the management tools available to them.

How, then, can the CEO bridge this gap? He or she must lead the marketing transformation through the craft of leadership. We talked to Tom Falk, CEO of Kimberly-Clark Corporation, about how he leads the marketing transformation to drive organic growth.

Tom Falk

In many ways, Tom fits the CEO mold we describe. After joining Kimberly-Clark in 1983, he spent most of his first ten years with the company in corporate finance. He was identified as a senior management candidate early in his career, which led to his attending Stanford University Graduate School of Business as a Sloan Fellow in 1988. Developmental assignments followed in manufacturing and supply-chain management.

He ascended quickly to a general-manager position leading the largest and most profitable group in the company. Subsequently he led the integration of the Scott Paper Company following the Kimberly-Clark/Scott merger in late 1995. He added geographic scope when charged with turning around the company's business in Europe. He was promoted to President and Chief Operating Officer and was elected to the company's board of directors in 1999. He became Chief Executive Officer in 2002 and Chairman in 2003. His rise to CEO involved a variety of experiences and achievements but did not include a stint in the marketing department.

Today, Tom successfully drives marketing transformation through four principles:

- Push growth boundaries beyond traditional limits.
- Create the ability to develop and apply insights.
- Apply positive risk management.
- Get the insights to market quickly.

Let's explore each of these so that you can see how to apply them to your organization.

Push Growth Boundaries Beyond Traditional Limits

Jack Welch, former CEO of GE, was famously quoted as instructing his managers that, whenever their businesses achieved a high share of their market, they should redefine that share to 10% or less by expanding the size of the market they were competing in. Similarly, Tom Falk and his team at Kimberly-Clark are working to expand the boundaries of their brands by creating new spaces in which they can compete.

Kimberly-Clark has some of the world's most trusted and recognized brands, including Kleenex and Huggies. For decades, the company has strived to make the best possible tissues and diapers and to persuade consumers worldwide to choose these brands over the competition. The company has worked with retail customers to maximize the effectiveness of shelf layouts and merchandizing schemes. Surely there must be a limit to the added growth that can be achieved over time with this focus.

Often, when such a barrier is reached, suboptimal decisions can be made. The consequences can erode the very brand equity that was accumulated over decades of brand building. Perhaps managers will drive the brand into increasingly marginal line extensions. Beverage brands, for example, often add flavors, each one with a narrower consumer appeal than the flavors that made the brand loved. These peripheral line extensions steal space on the delivery truck and space on the shelf from the established flavors. Because the purchase frequency and velocity on the store shelves are slower, the retailer becomes disillusioned with the brand's contribution to store revenues. The stocking clerk fills gaps in the established flavor shelf inventory with cans from the still-full case of the slow-moving flavor, exacerbating the deceleration in volume. It's a vicious cycle that's hard to break.

Pricing decisions often have similar consequences. Brand Managers will lower the price in an attempt to drive more volume. Yet, the value proposition to the consumer includes the prestige and reassurance that are built in to the premium price. Continuous price promotions confuse the consumer as to what the product is really worth. Cutting product costs and quality can have a similar effect. The cost reductions can increase the margin and bottom-line profit on a spreadsheet, but they may destroy the long-term value proposition built and reinforced in the consumer's mind by keeping a product quality promise.

Managers often make these decisions because they believe that there are boundaries to the growth of their current mature businesses. This leaves them with few options for "which levers to pull" to achieve revenue increases. Tom and his Kimberly-Clark leadership team set clear direction for where growth will come from, and then they remove or push out boundaries to growth.

Setting the Growth Strategy

"Our disciplined approach to growth is to look first at the organic growth that's possible from the businesses that we're already in and the brands we already own, and to get as much growth from those as we can. Organic growth is the highest return on investment available to any company. It is difficult, expensive, and risky to make acquisitions, and many never deliver the growth that's expected. So my approach is to focus on 'better is better' rather than 'bigger is better.' We should be clear about what we're trying to do with the business we're currently in, and that we're mining the growth that's there."

So how do you push out the growth boundaries that others perceive?

Moving the Boundaries

Tom explains the kind of thinking that moves boundaries for such long-established Kimberly-Clark brands as Kleenex and Huggies.

"There have been a lot of ideas suggested for products that could carry the Kleenex brand name. If we were to take a product-based view, we'd limit those ideas only to paper products. Yet, we know our consumers trust the Kleenex brand to care for their families across a wide variety of need states. Our challenge is to select the right insights to drive into the marketplace."

So what is the right formula for finding the new growth space for established brands? Kimberly-Clark uses the term "domain" to signify a new kind of brand footprint and emphasizes that the domain is defined by the consumer, not the manufacturer.

"What are the consumer's needs, and how do those growth spaces relate or connect to the brand idea? For example, looking at the diaper category, you can think about it as diapering, or maybe extend it to include toilet training, or even wiping. But if you really think about it from the consumer standpoint, it's about helping mom care for her baby. Her world includes shopping for clothing, baby formula, and other baby products. You may not want your brand to have entries in all those product areas, but how your products and brands relate to the overarching 'baby care' category is an important part of defining the domain."

Just opening up the organization's thinking in this way creates new *breadth*—a broader field in which to apply innovative ideas. Typically, these broader fields are multidimensional. For Huggies, for example, Kimberly-Clark created a new growth direction with a solution for moms whose babies were growing out of diapers:

"We've extended beyond diapers into products like Huggies Pull Ups training pants. It's another benefit our brand can provide moms as their children start toilet training. We've penetrated only about one-third of the U.S. market with this product. In other words, there are still big opportunities to take our brands, find new consumer solutions, and grow even in a well-developed market such as the U.S."

Similarly, the Huggies brand now offers a new range of toiletries and bath-time solutions for moms and their babies. This also demonstrates to Kimberly-Clark's retail customers how much new growth, revenue, profit, and shopper interest a brand like Huggies can bring them.

The leadership action of removing constraints has been the key to unleashing new growth from established brands.

Create the Ability to Develop and Apply Insights

Growth transformation does not require a massive and comprehensive management intervention. Usually, such interventions focus on changing the organizational structure and can cause major disruptions and a lot of turbulence before the new organization settles down. Tom Falk describes an approach that may be far less disruptive and more effective in providing the catalyst to drive growth.

The key to the transformation is the focus on insights. Insight generation is the beginning of the marketing value chain and, in fact, of the entire business value chain. If the leader focuses the entire organization on generating new insights into the needs of consumers and customers, a whole set of dominoes begins to fall in a virtuous sequence.

The first domino to fall is the realization that a new insight calls for a new set of solutions and that those solutions may come wholly or partially from outside the company.

"In the past, we tended to look to ourselves first for the solution and for the best practices. Today, we look outside as much as inside. We say to outside partners, 'Tell us your ideas on how you can deliver against this new consumer need state.'

We have the insight, we own the brand, we have the distribution access, we have the vision for where we want to take our business, and we use outside partners to help us deliver on the total solution. This doesn't mean we outsource all our solutions. There are some areas in the process where we clearly add unique value. But unbundling those activities, instead of saying we have to do them all ourselves, saves time. Some activities can happen in parallel, and some third parties are already well down the road to where we want to go. Let's partner with them and take advantage of their learning."

Another domino to fall is the realization that, with new insights, new kinds of talent are required to turn the insights into solutions, and new ways of tapping into that talent are required.

"There are many clever innovations at smaller companies where so much R&D is happening today. When I speak with young college graduates, including those with advanced degrees, fewer and fewer are going to work for big companies. They instead are going to work in start-ups and smaller companies. So how do you cast your net and find those smart people with great ideas and build relationships with them?

We're putting a lot of effort into building partnerships. We want to be a company that those talented people like to work with—a company that is easy to do business with, flexible enough to accommodate different styles and approaches. It's a good source of diversity and a great means of incorporating new ideas into our processes."

Not only is there a need to tap into new talent externally, there is also the need to rethink internal talent as soon as the new stream of insights starts to flow.

"We are certainly on the verge of radical changes in the way marketing career paths evolve. In the future, the talents and skills of people who choose marketing will be different and more diverse. The old approach to marketing is probably already dead: hire an MBA from one of the best schools; put them on a brand team; give them a big advertising budget.

"I think you will find more anthropologists, who really understand human behavior and how people connect with the world around them. You will find people with strong technology backgrounds who are adept at using interactive communication in their messages.

"The ways we apply marketing also will be different. If you think about a marketing team all working in the same building on a marketing project, that will change. Marketing will occur at customer locations and in retail environments. Those activities will be just as important as strategic brand building or traditional big-budget TV advertising.

"In short, we're going to see greater diversity of backgrounds coming into marketing and greater diversity of marketing work. There's still plenty of room for creativity and innovation within that space, but there'll be more science, more technology, and more measurement focused on the quality of the outputs, and not just the creativity of the inputs."

As soon as this insight-driven transformation starts to build, it influences all aspects of the organization and its activities and how they are connected and integrated.

"A consequence of becoming insights-driven is that everybody at Kimberly-Clark is now thinking about different and better ways to do things. We may not be able to do all of them, but our people are constantly thinking about ways to innovate. It becomes part of the DNA of a truly innovative company.

"Still, we can have a great insight, and we can turn it into an interesting product, but what good is it if we haven't prepared the ground from a customer standpoint? That is, if we don't know how to fit it on a shelf, or how to get it through a customer's supply chain. We are now building greater multifunctional capability to serve our customers. The work design connects our customer development organization with our product development organization for a seamless flow of ideas. The 'last mile' to the customer and then to the consumer is critical. That is a capability that you can't take for granted; it has to be right there at the start of the innovation process."

When you focus on insights, a transformation is set in motion that can change the entire organization and how it approaches all aspects of innovation. This includes how the organization translates insights into innovation, to how it delivers innovation to the marketplace, to the diversity of skills the organization assembles and the processes, to tools and technology it employs. Tom is convinced that the focus on insights and new ways of understanding consumer and customer needs and motivations is the right stimulus for transformational change.

"I believe that the insights-led transformation is evergreen; we are continually building our understanding of the consumer, building new insights and moving day by day into new opportunity areas. That's where the power of the insights process lies."

He maintains that conviction in spite of the "transformational idea of the day" mentality that sometimes pervades the management literature. Just as managing a brand requires a consistent message with innovative change in features and benefits, so does the building of the corporate transformation of the brand.

"An important element of transformation is consistency. You can't just read something in the Harvard Business Review or talk to a new consultant and change the agenda. You have to be consistent, and you have to reinforce the same message at every opportunity. Sometimes you can fall victim to saying, 'I shared my vision once; they know what I want, so they are going to deliver.' My experience reinforces how important it is to keep repeating the same, consistent message. It's much like building a brand. The act of transformation requires building an emotional connection with people in the organization. A CEO has to get people to believe in the transformation that there's an identified need; that there's reason to believe in the importance of meeting the need; that there's confidence in the organization's ability to deliver the solution; and that when it does, there will be a big win for everyone. If management can consistently communicate all those things, then people in the organization will embrace the transformation, they will want to pursue the mission, and they will adopt the new processes. The act of transformation uses our marketing skills as well."

Apply Positive Risk Management

Innovation is an inherently risky process. A financially astute CEO can look at risk in an operational and impersonal fashion without emotion. Risk can be quantified as a mathematical function and managed proactively, thereby reducing the fear factor.

Another way to proactively manage risk is to roll it up into a portfolio. A risk portfolio is simply a distributed set of possible returns. Some risks will be ranked high, low, or negative. If the portfolio is properly balanced, the manager can classify the "bets" with an optimum balance between big bets with higher returns and small bets with lower returns, along with high levels of opportunity for repetition and continuity. It's the proactive application of the risk model—analyzing past results to forecast future risk—that tames the beast.

Tom describes the risk portfolio as part science and part judgment.

"Part of senior management's role is to look at the funnel of ideas in the innovation pipeline and to select which of those ideas to fund. There are tools we can use such as real options pricing to help us determine which ones have the greatest potential for success. But the results from models like this are mostly directional. In the end, it comes down to management judgment about which ideas offer the most opportunity and then making the organization comfortable stretching to make those ideas a success."

Getting the organization to make that stretch requires culture change before behaviors change. Much has been written about culture change management, but Tom's view is very simple: make the organization comfortable with the requirements of risk management, including rapid decision making with incomplete information, and make good use of the learnings from those decisions.

"CEOs must clearly communicate the business results they want from the innovation process and how much they are willing to invest, and then throw their full support behind the investment and all its risks. It is also necessary to change behavior, and a critical part of doing so is how you treat failure. If the consequences for failure are punishment of the individuals involved, you are going to have an organization that's risk-averse. Yet innovation is an inherently risky process. So part of the transformation is building a process that forces decisions to be made in a timely manner. Thumbs up or thumbs down. This includes saying, 'You don't have permission to run another test, but you do have permission to make a decision based on the data in hand.'

"Similarly, there's an element of happily learning from failure—we followed the process, and it didn't yield the results that we wanted, so let's take stock of what we learned, improve it, and move on to the next opportunity. I tell our teams time and time again, 'If we don't fail once in a while, we're probably not trying enough new things.' Our teams are still learning to accept that. Not everyone believes it. Still, it is hard to find examples in our company today where people have been punished for taking a risk that failed."

Get the Insights to Market Quickly

The preceding discussion focused on the upstream components of the value chain—insights, innovation, development portfolios, and organizational capabilities. None of these are monetized until products and services are taken to market and consumers and channel customers pay for transactions. The growth-focused leader concentrates on the process to deliver innovation speedily into the marketplace. Tom Falk understands that insights can be unique and can create competitive advantage, but the advantage does not last forever and will eventually be diluted in a competitive market.

"You have to assume that your competitors understand the same or similar consumer insights. Once you have an insight, you can't patent it or lock it away very easily. That means within months of launching an innovation based on an insight, competitors may launch their own versions in other global markets. The functional benefits may differ, but others want to occupy that same space in the mind of a consumer. Developing a meaningful insight is an important step, but being able to quickly transform it into an innovation and quickly drive it into the marketplace are key elements as well."

How fast is fast enough?

"We are never satisfied with the speed we achieve. We're always trying to improve. We're more focused than ever on measuring cycle time consistently across the process, with a goal of continually reducing the time it takes from insights generation to marketplace launch."

How is it possible to improve? As soon as the idea of "growth as a process" is applied—insight generation inevitably leads to innovation in products, services, and business models—metrics and continuous improvement can be applied for greater speed and efficiency.

"We continually ask, what are the key decision points, and how can we accelerate getting to those decision points? All processes can be speeded up once you've mapped the decision points. For example, the conventional model can be speeded up by using the Internet as a tool for market research to get answers much more rapidly. But we can go even faster by changing the model—by getting the organization comfortable with taking a bit more risk—for example, going ahead without new research in cases where we already have great understanding of the consumer and their interactions with our products and our categories.

"We often can accurately predict the likely result of an insight or innovation without the delay of exhaustive testing. A good example is our recent restaging of Huggies Supreme diapers. We are relaunching the brand in North America and Europe at the same time. In the past, we would have launched it in one market or the other and waited to get a read on the results, and then fine-tuned it before taking it to the next market. Nowadays, you must be willing to introduce simultaneously in multiple geographies, and that means taking a bit more risk."

Leading the Way to Breakthrough Growth

Kimberly-Clark's approach highlights one of the most powerful aspects of the single-threaded end-to-end approach to growth. It begins with the generation of insights that feed multiple development streams:

- An innovation stream that drives toward new products and new services that make your brand, solution, or offering different and better than your competitor's

- A design stream that creates the consumer and customer experience that wins on relevance—"designed for me"—which is the second driver of marketplace effectiveness

✒ A branding and communications stream that builds the emotional bond with consumers and channel customers that makes them remain loyal to your offering

If you focus your organization on generating insights, the rest of the transformation will follow. Your teams will quickly realize that they need new solutions to deliver on the new insights. To generate the new solutions, they'll look for new partners and new resources. To manage the new ecosystem, they'll look for new skills, talents, and tools. They'll talk to customers differently. They'll organize processes differently and collaborate differently.

With this approach, the leader doesn't have to intervene to "change everything" in some massive restructuring. The leader simply uses these tools of leadership: identify the direction, remove the boundaries to growth, initiate the insight generation processes, and give the organization permission to take the risks needed to innovate and deliver the new solutions to market.

It is not easy. Nevertheless, the challenge of bringing new growth to established businesses can be approached systematically. The payoff is clear—stronger, more relevant brands; a new dialogue with retailers; and a deeper relationship with consumers.

Index

Marketing That Works
How Entrepreneurial Marketing Can Add Sustainable Value to Any Sized Company

LEONARD M. LODISH, HOWARD L. MORGAN, SHELLYE ARCHAMBEAU

The entrepreneurial marketing techniques, concepts, and methods the authors provide will help a venture make more money—extraordinary money—on a sustainable basis. The reader will be able to position and target their product/service offering to leverage their firm's distinctive competitive advantages, and make companies not only more effective in their marketing, but more efficient than their competition as well. The book begins by explaining the concepts of segmentation, positioning, targeted marketing, new product development, pricing, and distribution, all from the standpoint of an entrepreneurial marketer. It then goes on to explain how to create marketing efforts that will have greater impact, including relationship and brand management. If a venture is small, and needs to do a lot with a little, this book can show them how to make the most of their resources and get results that the larger companies will envy. If an organization is more established, this book is also for them, as they will find strategies that will allow them to reinforce relationships with their established stakeholders, and stretch the boundaries of their markets at the same time they stretch their dollar.

ISBN 9780132390750, © 2007, 336 pp., $29.99 USA, $33.99 CAN

Marketing Metrics
50+ Metrics Every Executive Should Master

PAUL W. FARRIS, NEIL T. BENDLE, PHILLIP E. PFEIFER, DAVID J. REIBSTEIN

Today's best marketers recognize the central importance of metrics, measurement, and accountability. But few marketers recognize the extraordinary range of metrics now available for evaluating their strategies and tactics. In *Marketing Metrics: 50+ Metrics Every Executive Should Master*, four leading researchers and consultants systematically introduce today's most powerful marketing metrics. The authors show how to use a "dashboard" of metrics to view market dynamics from various perspectives, maximize accuracy, and "triangulate" to optimal solutions. Their comprehensive coverage includes measurements of promotional strategy, advertising, and distribution; customer perceptions; market share; competitors' power; margins and profits; products and portfolios; customer profitability; sales forces and channels; pricing strategies; and more. You'll learn how and when to apply each metric, and understand tradeoffs and nuances that are critical to using them successfully. The authors also demonstrate how to use marketing metrics as leading indicators, identifying crucial new opportunities and challenges. For clarity and simplicity, they avoid advanced math: all calculations can be performed by hand, or with basic spreadsheet techniques. In coming years, few marketers will rise to senior executive levels without deep fluency in marketing metrics. This book is the fastest, easiest way to gain that fluency—and differentiate yourself in an ever more challenging environment.

ISBN 9780131873704, © 2006, 384 pp., $39.99 USA, $45.99 CAN